FASCINATING FORECASTS!

In a fierce and fascinating book this fabulous mystic, who warned spellbound TV audiences about the bombing halt, the power blackout, and the race riots, reveals startling facts about America's future.

AND MUCH MORE!

Here is the world of mysticism as Daniel Logan has lived it.

- The shameless phoneys who pose as mediums (with advice on how to spot them)
- The hair raising and heart warming experiences that led Daniel Logan to the Occult
- How YOU can develop the psychic talents that all of us possess

THE RELUCTANT PROPHET

DANIEL LOGAN

AVON
PUBLISHERS OF
DISCUS • CAMELOT • BARD

AVON BOOKS
A division of
The Hearst Corporation
959 Eighth Avenue
New York, New York 10019

First Avon Printing, October, 1969

AVON TRADEMARK REG. U.S. PAT. OFF. AND
FOREIGN COUNTRIES, REGISTERED TRADEMARK—
MARCA REGISTRADA, HECHO EN CHICAGO, U.S.A.

Printed in the U.S.A.

FOR CLARE, BILL, HYATO, CHRISTOPHER, ELIZA-
BETH, VALERIE, BARBARA SUE, KAREN, LEE
BARKER, MOTHER AND ALL THE OTHERS
WHO BELIEVED AND HELPED.

Author's Note

There have been many books about psychics and psychic phenomena. I hope, however, that this one will prove to be a bit different. Its purpose is not so much to prove the existence of a "psychic world"—mine or anyone else's—as it is to explain what it is like to be psychic and to record what effect my psychic gifts have had both upon me and upon those who have sought the aid of those gifts. For that purpose, it seemed that a personal, subjective approach was more suitable than an abstract and objective one; hence, the autobiographical format of this book. Moreover, psychic gifts and their exercise are an integral and important part of one's personality and one's life, and they are therefore difficult to explain, or to understand, outside of that context.

It is my hope, then, that this book will serve primarily to inform those who are already interested in the world of psychic phenomena. Perhaps it will also offer to the skeptical some evidence that such a world does, in fact, exist. With that latter use in mind, I have been careful to select for treatment in depth only those psychic consultations (or "readings")—out of the hundreds that I have given—that can be authenticated through the testimony of the person concerned.

Follow after charity, and desire spiritual gifts, but rather
that ye may prophesy.

For he that speaketh in an unknown tongue speaketh not
unto men, but unto God; for no man understandeth him;
howbeit in the spirit he speaketh mysteries.

But he that prophesieth speaketh unto men to edification,
exhortation, and comfort.

He that speaketh in an unknown tongue edifieth himself;
but he that prophesieth edifieth the church.

There are, it may be, so many kinds of voices in the
world, and none of them is without signification.

Wherefore tongues are for a sign, not to them that believe, but to them that believe not: but prophesying serveth
not for them that believe not, but for them that believe.

For ye may all prophesy one by one, that all may learn,
and all be comforted.

And the spirits of the prophets are subject to the
prophets.

If any man think himself to be a prophet, or spiritual,
let him acknowledge that the things I write unto you are
the commandments of the Lord.

—I Corinthians, XIV, passim

The age-old claims of psychic phenomena which have occurred in religion, metaphysics, and parapsychology tests can no longer be ignored. Almost daily, new horizons open up before science; gradually, the conclusion is being forced on us that mind, life, logos, spirit, or God is the only reality in this mysterious universe. The battle against the unknown is gradually being lost—or rather, won—by the new generation of scientists who are finding themselves more and more in Alice's Wonderland where nothing is impossible.

—Nandor Fodor

If I had my life to live over, I would be a parapsychologist. That is where the truth lies.

—Sigmund Freud,
shortly before his death, to Nandor Fodor

There are more things in heaven and earth, Horatio, than are dreamt of in your philosophy.

—Hamlet, Act One, Scene V

THE
RELUCTANT
PROPHET

1

November's early twilight had long since settled over the city, and through the window overlooking Madison Avenue I could see Manhattan twinkling almost cheerily through the smog. On the sidewalks below, secretaries and corporation vice-presidents, admen and office boys hurried home. For them, at least, the day's ordeal was over. But for me there was no relief in sight. Wearily I turned back to my inquisitor.

"I see you taking a trip," I said, sounding, and feeling, like a gypsy fortune-teller. "You will go to Europe on business."

He was unimpressed. "You could easily have read that in the newspapers."

I took a firm grip on my composure and on my patience. For the past several hours my psychic ability had been "on trial" in the offices of Mr. David Susskind, and I was exhausted, physically and emotionally. After having survived somehow an interminable gamut of questions, traps, and probings by staff members of the *David Susskind Show*, I was now facing Mr. Susskind himself, who is, by professional necessity more than by personal preference, the greatest skeptic of them all.

"This particular trip has something to do with a television show," I persisted, being painfully aware that just about anything Mr. Susskind did had something to do with a television show.

"There's no secret about that," Mr. Susskind responded predictably. "You could have heard it from any one of a hundred people."

"I see that most of the people involved in this production are men. But there is one female role, a very important one. Is that correct?"

17

He shrugged affirmatively, unconvinced that psychic gifts were necessary to uncover that bit of information.

"But here is something that neither I nor anyone else could possibly know without being clairvoyant. When you arrive in Europe, you will have a disagreement with the actress whom you have slated for that role. It will be a dispute over her billing. As a result, she will not do the show."

Mr. Susskind's expression, which had hitherto been one of firm if polite incredulity, now became one of undisguised disbelief. "That, my friend, is very hard to believe. The lady in question is Leslie Caron, and she is going to appear in my television production of *Dial M for Murder*. The show is going to be filmed in Europe next week, and the contracts have all been signed—including the contract with Miss Caron. She is a true professional about such things, and it's extremely unlikely that she would walk out after having signed the contract. Moreover, she likes the part very much. There is no problem, and I don't expect that there will be. So, there is no doubt that Miss Caron is going to do the show."

"I'm sorry," I answered. "I can't change what I see. The problem about billing *will* arise, and Miss Caron will *not* do the show. Then you will have another problem to face, that of selecting a replacement for her. There will be two candidates for the role. One will be a promising and talented younger actress, and the other an older, more experienced woman. After a great deal of thought and hesitation, you will give the part to the older actress. It will have been the right choice, for she will give an outstanding performance."

This conversation took place in November 1966. Two weeks later, I received a telephone call from Mr. Susskind.

"You were absolutely right about everything," he exclaimed. "I arrived in Europe to find exactly the situation you predicted. Miss Caron was in the middle of an argument about her billing status, and she did eventually refuse to do the show because of it."

I resisted a very human temptation to observe that I had told him so.

"But that's not all," Mr. Susskind continued. "What really amazed me was that everything else happened just as you said it would. We were put in a position where we had to choose between a younger and an older actress to replace Miss Caron—between Joanna Pettet and Diane Cilento. After much discussion, we chose Miss Cilento; and she certainly did give a great performance."

"Well, I'm glad everything turned out all right for you," I managed, with what I hoped was becoming modesty.

"To be perfectly frank, I didn't attach much importance to what you told me in my office that afternoon. But now I have to admit that you knew what you were talking about."

In addition to my predictions about Mr. Susskind's problems with his television show, several psychic demonstrations of a rather unusual nature had taken place in the Susskind offices on that November afternoon. One of them involved Don Silverman, an executive of the American Broadcasting Corporation who was visiting Mr. Susskind on another matter. I was urged to tell him "something psychic."

"Do you own a car?" I asked.

"No," Mr. Silverman answered without hesitation.

"You don't have a car—a blue car?"

This time, his "no" was hesitant.

"But you were driving a blue car recently. The impression is very clear. I know it was blue."

Abruptly Mr. Silverman's expression changed from perplexity to recollection. "Oh, my God, yes," he blurted out, and his face turned pale.

"You fell asleep at the wheel and lost control of the car for a moment. But you caught yourself just in time and barely missed having an accident."

"Yes," the now startled Mr. Silverman reiterated. "It happened just the other day. It was a rented car, and it *was* blue. I fell asleep just for a moment and woke up as I was heading off the road. But I haven't told a soul about it. In fact, I haven't even thought about it."

Word spread quickly around the Susskind suite that someone was doing an extraordinary "act" in one of the offices, and staff members began to drift in and ask for readings. One of them, Alan Shayne, talent director for Mr. Susskind's productions, asked if I could shed some light on a worrisome situation that was on his mind.

"You are wondering about a certain television series—whether or not it will get on the air. And you are worrying about what will happen to it if it does get on the air. Is that it?"

He nodded. "Can you tell me anything about what is going to happen?"

"I feel that it will get on the air eventually, but there will be many problems to be solved before that happens."

"Are they production problems? Sponsor problems?"

"Sponsor problems, mostly. The show you're thinking about is unusual—unusual in that it is very strong in content. Your prospective sponsors will object on those grounds. But I know that it will get on the air in spite of that."

"What kind of reception will it get?"

"Eventually it will be very successful. But, tell me, doesn't this show have something to do with men in uniform?"

"Yes," Mr. Shayne answered, "it does."

"And its title isn't composed of words. It's made up simply of letters of the alphabet."

"That's correct."

Another impression came to me quite vividly: the swastika. "Does the first segment in the series have anything to do with the Nazis?"

"Yes, it does. That's right."

Again I assured him that the series would get on the air. "But," I cautioned, "I see that you will have to do a great deal of editing and revising before that. In fact, almost half of what you have now will have to be cut before the series can be shown."

The series we were talking about was *N.Y.P.D.*, and had to do with the New York Police Department. At the time of that conversation, the project was still in its preliminary stages and no announcement about it had been made to the public. As it turned out, Mr. Susskind's staff did have a very difficult time getting the show on the air. The sponsors felt that the material was "too strong" or too controversial, and Susskind Productions was compelled to cut and edit until the running time of the show had been cut from one hour to thirty minutes. Finally the show premièred in the fall of 1967—and the lead actors were "in uniform."

Having satisfied the interest and curiosity of Mr. Susskind and his staff and, I hoped, proved myself an acceptable guest for Mr. Susskind's television show, I was preparing to leave when a lovely young lady entered the office in search of her father, Mr. Susskind. Introductions were made, and we fell into an informal discussion of psychic phenomena in general and of my psychic gifts in particular. Early along in our conversation, Miss Susskind, a woman of obvious intellectual endowment and interests, expressed the opinion that my clairvoyance consisted in reality of nothing more than a series of unusually fortunate guesses. And she was as unmoved by reports of what had occurred that afternoon as she was by my "guesses" concerning her own affairs.

Finally I attempted to confront her with evidence that she could not dismiss summarily. "You are having a romantic problem," I told her, again playing the gypsy. "You are having a disagreement with your boy friend."

"Mr. Logan," she said with studied patience, "I don't want to sound rude, but you could say that about almost any girl my age and it would probably turn out to be true."

I had to admit that she was correct on that score. But I had not yet finished. "This is a disagreement about something unusual—about skiing."

There was a pause. One could almost see the struggle between scientific detachment and the evidence of the senses. It is to Miss Susskind's credit that the latter gained the upper hand, and her doubt faded slightly. "That is precisely what we argued over," she admitted. "But how on earth could you know it?"

"I knew it because I *sensed* it to be so," I answered. "Which is very different from guessing."

"That's true," she conceded. "The odds against your guessing with such exactitude are astronomical. You could have chosen, or guessed at, any one of a million things that young people argue about. But you picked sports. And in that area you were able to narrow it down to skiing. It's remarkable."

It was obvious that Miss Susskind's scientific mind was

attempting to analyze a phenomenon of extrasensory perception and to assign to it a wholly rational—i.e., scientific—explanation. And I had the feeling that the young lady, torn between a mistrust of the "unscientific" and the value of the incontrovertible evidence offered, remained suspended somewhere between doubt and belief. In any case, when she eventually left the office after a long conversation, it seemed that her attitude toward psychic phenomena was no longer one of unalloyed disbelief.

Now that the ordeal, under both its formal and informal aspects, was over, I was told that I would indeed be invited to appear as a guest on Mr. Susskind's show. I say "ordeal" because such an exhaustive trial of one's psychic gifts is best described by that word. To undertake psychic demonstrations under the scrutiny of those who are interested—either personally or commercially—but who do not really believe or understand, is so debilitating as to leave the psychic exhausted, mentally and physically. The experience is comparable, I suppose, to that of a student who undergoes a three- or four-hour oral examination. It demands complete concentration and an alertness which, when maintained over a comparatively long period of time, require an extraordinary expenditure of energy. The student, of course, can depend on the examiners being thoroughly familiar with the field in which he is being questioned; but the psychic usually bears the additional burden of being interviewed by examiners who are qualified only by their curiosity and interest, and so he must spend much time and energy trying to explain some basic, but generally ignored, principles of psychic phenomena. Moreover, the psychic often finds that his examiners are not, to say the least, wholly in sympathy with what he is trying to do. It is not surprising, in view of what the psychic goes through on such occasions, that the whole subject of parapsychology and its phenomena has not been more thoroughly investigated by scientists. True psychics simply could not bear up under the strain of the examination that would be necessary. And add to that fact that psychics generally are painfully sensitive (which is probably more a cause than an effect of their gifts), and one can imagine with what anguish they would undergo any sort of intensive exploratory analysis.

My appearance on David Susskind's program was seen on network television in December 1966. It consisted of a short interview with Mr. Susskind, a few psychic observations with respect to individuals in the audience, and a series of predictions having to do with world affairs and events in this country. In those latter categories, some of my observations were as follows:

The greatest outbreak of racial violence in the history of the United States will take place during the summer of 1967. It will spread from New York to Los Angeles, and the northeastern and midwestern sections of the country will be the hardest hit. That year—1967—will be the crucial year in racial relations. After that, there will be a very gradual leveling off of tensions. In retrospect, 1967 will have proved to be the critical year.

(That prediction, unfortunately, was verified by the events of the summer of 1967. The most violent manifestations of racial strife during that violence-ridden summer took place in the northeast—Newark—and the midwest—Detroit. At the time that I made this prediction, it outraged certain civil-rights leaders. Such a thing, so those gentlemen said and wrote, could not and would not happen. One of those leaders was in the audience on the day that the show was taped, and he challenged me directly on-camera.)

The devastating drought in the northeastern part of the United States will end shortly. From the early part of 1967 through the fall of that year, there will be unusually heavy snowfalls, violent storms, and torrential rainfalls. Flood, rather than drought, will then become the problem, and I foresee flooding in many areas.

(In May 1967, because of unusually heavy snowfall during the foregoing winter and because of heavy rainfall, the drought did begin to abate. There were indeed floods in New York, Pennsylvania, Connecticut, and in North and South Carolina as well as in other eastern states.)

There will be a second electrical power failure in the eastern part of the United States, similar to the one that blacked out the northeastern part of the country in November of 1965. Following that, there will be a third, and finally a fourth such failure that will last for two days.

(In June 1967 there was a major power failure which affected sections of New Jersey, Delaware, and Pennsylvania. That was the "second" failure. The third and fourth failures are, as of this moment—i.e., November 1967—still in the future. It may be of incidental interest to mention here that I foresaw the blackout of November 1965.)

The winner of this year's Academy Award [i.e., that of 1966] will be Elizabeth Taylor.

(Miss Taylor did, of course, get the Award for her 1966 performance in *Who's Afraid of Virginia Woolf?*)

Then came matters of more importance for mankind at large:

The actual facts of the Kennedy assassination have not yet come to light, as I have maintained publicly several times in the past two years. There were three men involved in the actual shooting. Oswald did not act entirely "on his own," as the official report on the crime would have us believe. There were, in fact, three men involved. Another man, who was involved in some way, is a government official and he is presently in office. Eventually the entire truth about this crime will be made public.

The war in Vietnam will increase in intensity. It will not remain confined to Vietnam but will infect many areas of southeast Asia. There are those who predict that the end of this war is in sight, but that is not the truth. The war will actually last for many years yet. Eventually—that is, within the next twenty years—the war in southern Asia will bring the United States to the brink of a major war.

I also made other predictions during this program, but the above were the most significant ones. Each of these will be discussed at length later, and I will try to explain at that time how the "psychic impressions" on which they are based were arrived at.

At first, I was rather disappointed with my appearance on the *David Susskind Show*. It seemed too brief—my total time "on" was twenty-five or thirty minutes, including commercials—and far too bland, too cut-and-dried, for it to accomplish what I had intended; that is, to awaken public interest in the question of clairvoyance. Yet, I was aston-

ished (and, I confess, more than a little pleased) to find
that, from the moment that the show was aired, my whole
life took a new direction. In the years previous, I had
sought success, both financial and personal, in many different areas, and I had almost inevitably experienced failure and disappointment. Now, suddenly, success was
sprung on me simply by virtue of a half hour spent before
a television audience. I awoke, as it were, to find myself at
least known, if not famous—and known as a clairvoyant, as
a psychic. The paradox inherent in this situation was that
I, who had sought fame in so many directions, had never
for one minute wanted to be known as a psychic medium,
and I had never had any desire to follow that calling as a
career. Far from seeking it out, I had done my best to
resist it, and for years I had fought this mysterious gift
both consciously and subconsciously. Finally, however, it
overtook me. There was, it seems, no other door for me to
pass through. And, as I look back, it becomes obvious that
this door has always been there, waiting for me to take a
first step beyond it into an unexplored and often fantastic
realm.

Pushed by circumstances, and perhaps impelled by fate,
I have taken that step.

2

Hartford, Connecticut, seems an unlikely place in which to
be introduced to the world of the psychic. Yet, it was
there, in June of 1957, that I received the first indication of
the course that my life was to follow. I had come to
Hartford from New York City on the basis of an offer of
employment as a ballroom-dancing instructor. After a less-
than-spectacular career as an actor in New York, this new
job seemed to promise, in addition to a comfortable salary,
the opportunity for a certain amount of artistic expression

and, just as important, a certain amount of stability in my life. In a short time, however, the job proved to be a fiasco on all counts, and I was forced to turn to those less congenial forms of employment that out-of-work theater people know so well, such as selling in department stores. Desperately lonely and engaged in work that I loathed, I was miserable.

During the six months that I spent in Hartford in those uncomfortable circumstances, I made one close friend, Mrs. Mae Aitken, a kindly lady now in her seventies. It was not, for me, an unusual relationship despite the difference in our ages. As a child, I had gravitated toward older people and they, for some reason, toward me.

Mrs. Aitken was a lady with a serious turn of mind, and it was during one of our countless discussions on philosophy, religion, and self-awareness that she let it be known that she was a Spiritualist.

I had never heard the term before.

"Spiritualists," Mrs. Aitken explained, "believe in a life after death, and in that they are like the members of most other churches. But they also believe in the ability of souls of dead persons to communicate with the living. This is done through persons who have certain talents, or gifts, and we call such persons 'mediums,' since they act as intermediaries between the living and the dead. The mediums receive information from the souls of the dead, and they pass it on to those who are still alive."

It all seemed a bit spooky, and frightening. I was intrigued, and even interested, but wary of what had all the earmarks of being a sect of "nuts." This lady, I thought, has got to be a little unbalanced, so intense was her belief in what she was explaining. Still, bored with my daily routine and frustrated by a budget which made no allowances for entertainment, I could not resist Mrs. Aitken's invitation to accompany her to a forthcoming Spiritualist meeting.

The following Sunday was a hot, humid June day. Somewhat regretting my acceptance, I escorted my friend to the First Spiritualist Church, located on Hartford's Park Street. The church, which was actually a converted two-room apartment, seated approximately fifty people and most of the chairs were already occupied when we arrived. We took chairs near the door—and I had an over-powering urge to leave immediately. The whole idea seemed suddenly ridiculous—spirits, mediums, ghosts, ouija boards, seances; this was for lonely old ladies with nothing better to interest them, not for a sophisticated, reasonably hip young man of twenty-one. Nonetheless, it would certainly have embarrassed, and perhaps irritated, my friend had I insisted on leaving, so I said nothing.

Within a few moments of our arrival the ceremonies began, presided over by one Reverend Doucette and his wife. The first part of the service was perfectly ordinary and followed the pattern common in most Protestant churches: hymns, a sermon, the collection, and prayers. At one point, candles were distributed to the congregation and, having been lighted, were placed on the rostrum in memory of departed loved ones. Heat from the flames sent the temperature up to, I am sure, over ninety. Feeling hot and faintly sick, I decided to brave Mrs. Aitken's displeasure and nudged her, motioning toward the exit. But at that moment Reverend Doucette announced the principal (and, to me, unorthodox) part of the service: the giving of "psychic messages." This was what I had come to see. My discomfort notwithstanding, we remained in our seats.

The minister introduced the medium, a middle-aged, crippled woman who mounted the rostrum. There was no trance, no hokus-pokus of any kind. The woman simply spoke out in a normal voice and tone, giving short messages "from the spirit world" to various members of the congregation. These messages were all different from one another, and apparently tailored to the requirements and problems of the individual addressed. One member was told about a sum of money she had lost. Another was informed about an event in her proximate future. A third was advised concerning her health. And so on. The members receiving messages all seemed to find them perfectly reasonable and in conformity with the circumstances of their lives.

My conclusion at that time was that the medium came to this church often, and that she knew personally each of the members of the small congregation. Thus, she was able easily enough to keep abreast of their personal problems and circumstances. To me, it seemed quite easy to figure out—and there was nothing supernatural or "spiritual" about it.

I was congratulating myself on my perspicacity when the medium singled me out for her attention. "I want to speak to that young man in the back, near the door."

Embarrassed beyond words, I slouched down and pretended not to hear.

"Yes, I mean you, young man," she persisted in a loud voice. "Don't try to hide. And don't leave, as I know you've been thinking of doing. This may be your first Spiritualist meeting, but it's not going to be your last."

Little does she know, I thought.

"Young man, you're going to be quite famous some day."

I was pleased with that. Maybe there was something to all of this, after all.

"Now, hold on. It's not going to be in the way that you're thinking. As a matter of fact, you're going to become famous by doing exactly the kind of work that I'm doing up here today."

I uttered a disbelieving grunt. The lady's prophecy was so farfetched as not to be worth considering.

"Don't doubt me, young man," she went on, obviously accustomed to skepticism. "You are going to be known as one of the most famous psychics of your time."

The congregation turned en masse to see this rising star. Shocked and embarrassed, I wanted desperately to leave. But I was held to my seat by the knowledge that flight would simply make me more of a spectacle than I already was. Then anger began to replace embarrassment. How dare that woman say such nonsense? It was unbelievable, absurd, unimaginable. If she was so "sensitive," why couldn't she sense the very real inner torture that I was enduring? Why couldn't she see now unbearable it was to be blocked in everything that I had attempted? Complete strangers had told me that they could sense that I was a born actor. Couldn't this self-appointed medium tell me something about that? Why did she make up this gibberish about being a famous psychic? It would only add to the frustration of not being able to succeed at what I really wanted to do.

But the medium went on relentlessly, apparently unaware of my rising resentment. "Within the next ten years, you'll be on top. You'll reach millions of people through radio and television. Your star will climb high in the psychic world."

Oh, God, I thought. What a fake. I was right in the first place. She doesn't know me, and so she has to make up something to say—something so fantastic that it will be credible. With that explanation I was satisfied, though still irritated. And apparently the medium also was satisfied in her own way, for she went on to the next member of the congregation for whom she had a message.

At Mrs. Aitken's insistence, we remained after the service for a few minutes so that I could "meet the congregation." It was not a meeting that I was especially looking forward to. Many of the members—in fact, a disproportionately large number of them—were rather strange-looking. They were strangely dressed, in garments that bespoke a total disregard for fit, color or fashion. Their bizarre appearance was not enhanced by that peculiarly abstracted look that settles upon people who have divorced themselves from the material world and taken refuge in a "higher reality"—whether that reality be religion (orthodox or otherwise), drugs, liquor, madness, or politics. It is a characteristic, in a word, of the True Believer of any persuasion. I was too lacking in experience to know it then, but these idiosyncrasies are typical of Spiritualists in general. Now, to make things worse, these odd people were staring at me, no doubt believing, as a revealed truth from the other world, that they were gazing upon a future luminary of the occult. I wanted to get out in a hurry.

My exit was forestalled by the acting medium, who came over to me and shook my hand. "God bless you," she said, "and may He bless the work that you'll be doing."

I forced a weak "thank you."

Leaving the First Spiritualist Church of Hartford, I vowed never to return and never again to be in the presence of self-appointed mediums and their so-called psychic impressions.

This was not to be. Obviously I was not much of a prophet at that time.

3

To be a practicing psychic in the twentieth century—a century devoted, above all things, to the exploration of the physical universe—is an anomalous situation. Yet, that condition is, to a certain extent, the story of my life. It began on April 24, 1936, in Flushing Hospital, New York City, where I was born—dead.

At two o'clock that morning, my mother's labor pains had begun. A nurse, answering her call, discovered that childbirth was in progress and also that all of the hospital's delivery rooms were already occupied. The only solution that the woman was capable of devising was to retard delivery until a room became available. This she did by the simple expedient of forcing the child—i.e., me—back into the womb whenever it was beginning, by purely natural means, to emerge into the world. Hours later, a specialist happened upon the scene and rushed the collapsing mother to a delivery room. There, he extracted from my mother an apparently lifeless form.

"It's dead," he whispered to the attending nurse.

But his *sotto voce* verdict did not escape my mother. "Oh, no! He's not dead! Do something! Don't let him be dead!"

The doctor, doubtless more to satisfy my mother than from any real hope of saving the child, went into action. He began slapping the motionless baby. For a long while, there was no response; but the slapping continued. Then suddenly the black and blue infant began to cry. I had, quite literally, been beaten to life.

Despite such an unpromising beginning, I am told that I was a fairly well-behaved baby. I'm glad of that, for my family had already had its share of hardship. Both my parents are second-generation immigrants of Czechoslovakian descent. (I was born George Daniel Olaschinez. I took the surname Logan when I began working in the theater. Who could pronounce Olaschinez?) They were both born in New York City, slightly after the turn of the century. When my mother, whose name was Teresa Huha, was three years old, her mother, homesick for the "old country," took her children back to Czechoslovakia—which was then part of the Austro-Hungarian Empire—for a visit. While they were there, World War I broke out. Since Austria-Hungary formed part of the Central Powers, they were trapped, so to speak, behind enemy lines. My mother was not to see the United States again until she was eighteen years old. After the war, the great influenza epidemic broke out, and Grandmother Huha and one of her sons were among its victims.

Shortly thereafter, Grandfather Huha returned to his family in Czechoslovakia, which, by now, comprised only my mother and her two brothers. My grandfather had just retired as an engineer for the New York City Transit Authority. During the years of his employment with the Authority, he had himself given ample evidence of certain psychic gifts. There were then (as now) many insurance claims against the Authority, and it was Grandfather Huha's ability to be able to tell immediately whether or not the claimant was faking in order to collect the insurance money. Over a period of years, his talent for separating the sheep from the goats was found to be nearly infallible.

In addition to this commercially useful gift, Grandfather Huha later showed a penchant for clairvoyance. Reunited with his family in Czechoslovakia, he discovered that he was able to foresee events in the lives of his relatives and neighbors. He claimed that he had received this information "from a gypsy" on his trips to town. But my mother swears that her father would make predictions even when he had not left the house for many days. Apparently a fear of being suspected of witchcraft or of possessing "diabolical powers"—no laughing matter in old Czechoslovakia—prevented his admitting that he was clairvoyant.

Years passed. Grandfather Huha died, and his sons and daughter again began the painful process of immigration to America. Once here, my mother, being now an orphan, was cared for by distant cousins named Olaschinez. My father was a member of that family and, to make a long story short, the two young people met, fell in love, and were married.

My father, as a young man, was a person of many talents and many ambitions. Despite those gifts, however, and despite his will to succeed, he was constantly frustrated in attempting to reach the goals that he set for himself. While he was a young bachelor, for example, a famous motion-picture company set up a production studio near the Olaschinez home in Whitestone, Long Island. Father was employed by this studio as a carpenter, stagehand, technician, and, eventually, as an actor. In the latter capacity, he played small roles in many films. When the company moved to Hollywood, however, he was prevented by a domineering mother from following it, and a promising, or at least rewarding, career had to be abandoned. Similarly, he could have been successful as a professional football player or bowler, having played spectacularly on semiprofessional teams in both sports. Such careers, however, are highly speculative and uncertain in their initial stages, and a married man with two children must have a steady, reliable income. (That was before the day of the six-figure "bonus" for promising professional players.) So, my father was forced to turn to manual labor and, for most of his life, his talents notwithstanding, he has been a laborer.

Father, having never reached the heights he had hoped for in his youth and having had to settle for far less, resigned himself to life with ill-concealed resentment. My mother, for her part—probably because of the great hardships she had experienced in Europe—became highly emotional and sensitive. Between her nervousness and my father's smoldering dissatisfaction, the moments of peace and tranquility in the Olaschinez home were rare. Hardly a day passed without a clash of some kind.

The connection between the tensions of this domestic situation and the development of my psychic gifts are, at least to me, obvious. Most people believe that psychics are born, not made. To a certain extent, that is probably true. But it is equally true, I believe, that most people are born with some potential psychic talent. There are conditions in which this latent ability is given the opportunity to develop—conditions, in other words, in which the child must fall back on his own internal strengths and abilities. And there are conditions in which the child remains unaware of his gifts, so that they remain dormant. I am convinced that, in my own circumstances, my childhood environment—the conflict, the tensions, the emotional upsets—contributed greatly toward the evolution of my awareness of the feelings of others, which is an indispensable factor in the operation of a psychic talent. An artist of any kind is born with a gift, but his gift is formed and brought into focus by the effects of conditions in the early years. The same is true of psychic ability, which, after all, is a talent much as, say, an ear for music or a sense of color.

In retrospect, it seems that I was placed in a position in which this awareness or sensitivity was forced to grow constantly. One such cause was the feeling of intense competition and mutual resentment which existed between my elder brother and me. More often than not, this feeling was expressed violently and explosively. I was a bookreading, introverted, and quiet child. My brother, on the other hand, was a normal, red-blooded all-American male—the kind of boy that any father dotes on. And, in fact, there was not a time in childhood when this difference between my brother and me was not being pointed out to me by my parents, or when I was not constantly being urged to emulate him. My brother, of course, formed by our parents' attitudes, could not abide his nonsportive, slightly built, and withdrawn sibling. The other children in the neighborhood were, for the most part, my brother's age and my brother's friends. And even when I attempted (against better judgment) to take part in their games and sports, I was laughed off the field for my clumsiness and inadequacies.

My father is hardly the sort of man to whom an unhappy child could appeal for understanding. Raised in the tradition of the Old World, he was not a demonstrative man. And he was much too busy earning a living to find the time, or to expend the energy, to guide his children. I cannot recall his ever having comforted me, or, for that matter, given any outward expression of love.

Once, I hated him for this. But I have since come to understand his frustration and bitterness. I can now understand his resentments, his unhappy resignation, and his inability to communicate.

In many respects, my mother is the complete opposite of my father. For that reason, it was equally impossible to communicate with her. She was affectionate, it is true; but she was also extremely high-strung, emotional, and domineering. An overture on my part was as apt to be greeted by a tantrum as by sympathy.

It is small wonder that, in those circumstances, I became "nervous" (as it was called then) at a very young age. I was moody and generally uncommunicative, subject to fits of depression, and I cried at the slightest provocation or with no provocation at all. This hypersensitivity was, quite naturally, subject to ridicule by relatives who lived in the neighborhood. They probably felt that, by teasing and making fun, they would force me to outgrow this disagreeable "phase" quickly.

Such treatment, as might be expected, had an effect quite opposite to the one intended and, as I grew older, I became more and more withdrawn. The situation was further complicated, when I was nine, by the birth of another brother. As years went by, it became clear that my younger brother was like the elder, and the two entered into a natural alliance against me. There were constant unkind references, in the cruel manner of children, to my physical appearance, to my sensitivity, and so forth. The alliance was blessed by my relatives, who often took my brothers on trips and vacations but left me at home because I was "too nervous to have around."

Unable to find the understanding and love that children usually expect from family relationships, I was forced to look for them in worlds of my own creation. First and foremost, there were pets. I kept every conceivable kind of domestic, or domesticable, animal as a pet. And I attribute my survival of childhood, in large part, to the opportunity afforded by these pets for a mutual exchange of love and of the feeling of being needed.

Of course, I also daydreamed constantly, and in these daydreams I always saw myself as an adult in a career in which, by ministering to those around me, both their lives and mine would be better. In those moments of escape, as in real life, I often cast myself in the role of a doctor or of a priest, since those professions seemed to me to be ideally suited for anyone whose ambition it is to be of service to mankind. But, as I grew older, I realized that I lacked the scientific turn of mind necessary for medicine, and the patience and self-discipline required for the religious life.

One afternoon, my mother took me to see a motion picture. It was a comedy, and everyone around us laughed a great deal and seemed to be having a wonderful time. I became lost in the make-believe world that the actors conjured up. Suddenly I knew what I wanted to be: an actor. Subconsciously, I suppose, I felt that before an audience I would find the admiration and respect that was denied me at home. It is axiomatic that actors are mostly people who feel they have to prove their right to live. On the conscious level, however, it seemed to me that, as a performer, I could be of some use and value in the world by making people laugh and forget their troubles.

Even at that early age, it was obvious to me that I was laboring under several disadvantages that I would have to overcome if I were ever to become an actor—or at least a successful one. Chief among these was my timidity. I was excruciatingly, unbelievably shy, so much so that I found it almost impossible to speak coherently to strangers. How, then, could I ever hope to climb up on a stage to speak before hundreds of strangers? This handicap obviously had to be conquered, and I set about the task with a will. The easiest way seemed to be to present myself as something that I was not, and, like the actors in the first film I had ever seen, I hid behind the mask of comedy. As most novices do, I overplayed the role outrageously and my antics were, I confess, often more obnoxious than engaging. But this self-devised therapy worked, and before very long I began to emerge from my shell. Soon, I had gained the attention of the only audience that really matters to a schoolboy, his classmates. From then on, I made a farce of everything. Nothing was too sacred to escape. My schoolmates wanted to be around the "school clown" to see what I would do next. I quickly became a pet nut, as it were, and I was accepted into the social life of the school strictly on that basis. Meanwhile, my true feelings continued to burn within, and I longed to be able to drop the mask and present myself as I really was. But I did not dare take the chance and risk being ignored again.

It was in high school that I first became aware of a certain psychic ability. I could, for example, predict which boy would date which girl before either of them had ever thought of it. On one occasion, I had the poor judgment to tell a classmate that his parents would soon be divorced. The boy was justifiably furious, and he launched into a tirade explaining how happy his parents were together. About a year later, the boy's mother and father separated and, eventually, were divorced. My friend was puzzled; he could not understand how I had known this a year beforehand. And I could not explain, for I did not understand it any more than he did.

Not only did I not understand this ability, but I was also frightened by it. I had no idea of where this mysterious information came from, what it was, or what to do with it. Having been raised a Catholic and thus having heard of cases of diabolical possession, I thought it might possibly all be the work of the Devil—something I was reluctant to be associated with, to understate the case. Thus, when these impressions, this strange knowledge, came into my mind, I usually tried to think of other things immediately.

When I finished high school I had my heart set on going to college to study dramatic arts. My parents, however, would not hear of it. "You can go to college," was their decision, "only if you choose a practical subject, as your brother did." My brother was studying education and intended to become a teacher. That was not the kind of life that I envisioned for myself. I decided that if I could not go to college, the next best thing was to move to Manhattan and try to get work in the theater.

The story of my life in Manhattan followed the well-known and worn pattern of youth trying to "make it" in the theater: work in little-theater groups, off-Broadway shows, small nightclubs, and, above all, those extremely frequent and interminable periods of being "between engagements." For all the excitement and satisfaction of being in a show, in no matter how small a role, no matter how far off Broadway, no matter how amateurish, it is not the engagements, but the periods in between engagements that allow the struggling young actor to make a living. Again, my life followed the classic pattern. During those years, I was employed, at one time or another, as a waiter, a postal clerk, a theater usher, a secretary, a salesman, an animal trainer—and a dozen other occupations, too numerous (and too mundane) to list. Eventually I found that I had reached the actor's dark night of the soul: I was absolutely unable to secure theatrical employment of any kind.

It was at this point that the dance-studio job in Hartford presented itself, and I was more than ready to accept. The promise of a fresh start, a new atmosphere, and a stable life was both new and exciting. When the studio failed, therefore, I felt entirely lost. Desperately missing New York and my friends there, and deprived in Hartford even of the remotest chance of getting a theater role of any kind, I was stranded without money, without a job, and with what seemed to me a mountain of debts.

Had I not been in such desperate circumstances, I doubt that I should have so readily taken up Mrs. Aitken on her invitation to attend that first Spiritualist meeting. And had I not gone along with her, then I should very likely never have become interested in the psychic world. Looking back, it seems that my footsteps were being guided quite firmly, by what ostensibly was chance and coincidence, onto the path that I was to follow.

4

My encounter with psychic phenomena at the Hartford Spiritualist Church had, as one may imagine, unnerved me. For days I went about brooding over the medium's prediction and attempting to convince myself that the whole thing was irrational and, therefore, preposterous.

Yet, I was haunted by the memory of the psychic impressions I had received as a student, episodes which my recent experience had recalled vividly to mind. Finally, I was able to persuade myself that Spiritualism was without any foundation in truth—but, at the same time, I wanted to know more about the accurate predictions that I myself had been able to make in years past. I discussed this with Mrs. Aitken, and she suggested that I have a "private reading" with a well-known medium in Windsor Locks, a town adjoining Hartford.

The medium's name was Martha. She lived in an old apartment house on the outskirts of the city. Her rooms were filled with ancient, dilapidated furniture, and tattered, colorless rugs covered the floors. The whole place impressed one as having been neglected for years. The rooms were darkened, and the fumes of burning incense floated on the musty air. A candle flame flickered in one corner of the room. It was an atmosphere that I was to find duplicated many times in the quarters of other mediums.

While we waited for Martha, Mrs. Aitken briefed me on her. Martha had been released from jail only a week previously. She had been arrested and sentenced for giving a reading to a policewoman (who was *incognita*, of course) and asking for a fee. It was not the reading itself that constituted a criminal act, but the asking for a fee. In many states, Connecticut and New York included, it is against the law to practice fortune-telling, prophecy, mediumship, or occultism of any kind for profit. And the operative term here, obviously, is "for profit." So long as one does not charge a fee or ask for a "donation," one may do what one will with impunity. For this reason, many psychics affiliate themselves with Spiritualist churches as ordained ministers. This is usually done not out of religious zeal, or even out of belief, but solely for protection. Since Spiritualism is an organized, legally recognized religion, its ministers cannot be arrested for accepting offerings from the faithful in return for the exercise of their ministry. Martha, in fact, was going to receive her papers as a Spiritualist minister within the week, and thenceforth she would be able to share her gift, for profit, without further harassment by the police.

Martha was, I discovered when we met her, a card-reader. That is, she operated by turning over a certain number of cards from a deck of playing cards; each card was supposed to have a different, and personal, meaning for the individual getting the reading. It was "fortune-telling" in the popular sense of the term. To me, it seemed merely a game of chance. For, after the cards were shuffled and chosen, the same cards would turn up regardless of who was having the reading, and the visitor, be he policeman or the president of Indonesia, would find that his fortune was exactly the same as that of anyone else who might have been there at the time of that particular shuffle and that particular dealing of the cards.

Despite these reservations about Martha's modus operandi, I was intrigued when I noticed that, occasionally, she would say something without looking at the cards. At one point, looking up from the cards and, staring blankly past my shoulder, she said, "I see you back in New York in the near future. You will be employed in the kind of work you want to do soon after you arrive there. I see you dressed in a uniform. You are with other men, and they also are in uniform. You seem confined to a small area. It is very cold. You have on a long coat. Whatever this is, it will not succeed, but it will lead to more rewarding things."

Most of what Martha saw that day in the cards never materialized. But what she saw when she was not looking at the cards did take place with startling accuracy. Within a month's time of the reading, I returned to New York City. After trying out for several roles, I was assigned a part in an off-Broadway production called *There Is No End*, a prisoner-of-war drama. It had an all-male cast, in uniform. The action of the play confined us to the area of the prison barracks during what was supposed to be a bitterly cold winter, and I wore a long trenchcoat throughout the show. And *There Is No End* was indeed a failure, but it did pave the way for more work.

The fulfillment of this one prediction of Martha's convinced me that, at those times that she was not trying to make sense out of the purely fortuitous turn of a card, she was actually receiving impressions similar to the one that had come to me concerning the divorce of my school-friend's parents. The proof of it seemed to be that this had been the only accurate prediction that Martha made, and the only one that she made independently of the cards.

Martha's detailed description of this incident aroused an even greater desire in me to learn more about psychic phenomena. It did not matter that most of what Martha had foreseen never transpired. That one remarkable accurate prediction was enough to pique my interest once and for all.

I began my search for knowledge in the only place that I knew of, the Spiritualist Church. To my surprise, there were many of them listed in Manhattan's Yellow Pages. I selected one located in the complex of studios and apartments in the Carnegie Hall Building, and I attended the next service there, which was on a Wednesday afternoon. It was the custom of the church's minister, the Reverend Frances Parker, to hold "open house" on Wednesday afternoons, when psychic consultation would be available to all who sought it.

The room in which these receptions were held was quite small, but adequate for the purpose since only a few people attended. Reverend Parker sat facing the group and, after a few moments of meditation, she would drift off into what appeared to be a trancelike state. At that time, anyone could ask whatever question he wished, or could describe whatever problem on which he wanted the medium's advice. Miss Parker's insights were generally of a spiritual nature, and it is difficult to judge either the accuracy or the value of those. But the material guidance that she gave—and that seemed to be what most of the people had come for—tended to be what the person asking wanted to hear rather than what would eventually take place in reality. I myself, for example, got into difficulty more than once simply by following Reverend Parker's advice with respect to my theatrical career.

I attended these Wednesday-afternoon seances several times. On my last visit, Reverend Parker told me, in response to an innocuous question, "You could very well receive your own psychic thoughts."

I confessed that I had, on occasion, done just that; but that I had no control over these thoughts—that they came and went seemingly of their own volition.

"You must go inward," Reverend Parker said, "and seek your true path. You must meditate daily. You must discipline your thinking and your material life."

"How should I go about doing that?" I asked.

"The way will be made known to you. Have patience. Have faith. The time is not right now, but it will come in the future."

I vaguely knew of the "higher teachings" about which Reverend Parker spoke, and I had seen enough of the literature of the Spiritualist churches to be generally aware of what was involved. The trouble was, I was far too lazy to study, and too lackadaisical to be willing to discipline myself in any way. I simply wanted a miracle to occur which would bring about the change in my life and in my luck that I wanted.

With such an attitude, it is no wonder that I soon found myself once again in dire financial straits and was forced to take a temporary job outside of the theater. This time, it was with the concession department of Radio City Music Hall, New York City.

At Radio City I soon got to know one of the managers in charge of the concessions, William McCarthy. As it turned out, he was also quite interested in the occult and had studied Christian Science and related teachings. We became fast friends at once, and we have remained so ever since.

After I had been with the concession department for a short time, William invited me to attend a Christian Science meeting. While I was skeptical about the principles and practices of Christian Science itself, the overriding impression that I carried away with me from that meeting was of the goodness and love which flowed from every church member present. They seemed the most content group of people that I had ever met. My subsequent, limited contact with that church and its members has not altered that impression.

Shortly before Christmas in 1960, I invited William, along with Mrs. Aitken, who was visiting New York, to come to my apartment for a seance. I had been reading books on the occult, and I was determined to have my first formal contact with the psychic world. I had received "messages" before without any effort on my part, and I could not see why I should not be able to do so, as it were, on cue. The method I had determined to use was to go into a trance. I had read about Edgar Cayce and others who had done this sort of thing, and I thought it an intriguing challenge.

We prepared the room in the classic manner: lights off, draperies drawn, candles lighted, incense in the air, and, for background, a record of religious music on the phonograph. Stretching out on the sofa, I concentrated on the glowing flame of a candle. Nothing happened. A great amount of time seemed to pass. I felt relaxed, but there seemed to be nothing out of the ordinary happening. Then, the flickering of the candle flame began to have a strange effect on me. I was being hypnotized; or, perhaps more accurately, I was hypnotizing myself. Brilliant colors flashed before my eyes. The room spun. I was out.

The next sensation of which I was aware was that of cold water running over me. Indeed, that is exactly what was happening. William and Mrs. Aitken were standing over me, calling my name and preparing to douse me again. It took some time before I was completely myself, and the process involved periods of near-hysteria on my part. When I had some control of my senses again, William explained what had taken place. I had gone into what appeared to be a trance, with the usual symptoms of that state; that is, I was oblivious to my surroundings, and my voice had changed to the extent that I sounded like a completely different person. I had given William and Mrs. Aitken information of a personal nature as well as on public affairs and on the international situation. All told, I had been "out" for approximately a half hour.

When I had stopped talking, my friends had waited a few minutes, expecting me to come to on my own. As time passed, however, I showed no signs of doing so, and they became alarmed and tried to rouse me. They shouted at me, tried to make me drink water, and even struck me. There was absolutely no response. Then they carried me into the shower and ran cold water over me. Finally, under the shock of the cold water, I began to revive.

It was, on the whole, a horrifying experience, and it was to be several years before I could again get up the courage to attempt to operate in a trance.

Among the predictions I made on that occasion, according to my friends, were several concerning future events in the area of international relations. I forecast, for example, that, although the Soviet Union and the United States were at that time (1960) in cutthroat competition, they would, before 1975, enter into a formal alliance. The threat to both of them at that time would not be, as in the past, one another, but Red China. As a result of this situation, I saw that a major confrontation, and very possibly a major war, would occur between the United States and China in the 1980's. I also disclosed that a number of catastrophes would set back the (then) newly inaugurated space program of the United States.

On a personal level, I warned Mrs. Aitken of the imminent loss of a beloved brother from a cardiac condition, unless he could be persuaded to rest and care for himself. Mrs. Aitken was taken aback by this, and she said that she was quite certain that her brother had no record of any heart trouble. The following year, however, Mrs. Aitken's brother died of a heart attack.

For myself, I do not remember anything that happened during the trance, nor do I recall any of the prophecies reported by my friends. William told me, however, that I said nothing at all concerning my own situation then or about my future. I have learned since that this is par for the course. It is rare that a psychically gifted person is able to utilize his talents on his own behalf.

In the weeks following this "seance" I became increasingly preoccupied with the significance of what I had thus far accomplished with my life. Or, frankly, I became more and more concerned with the significance of what I had not accomplished. Time was passing swiftly, and I had, in fact, despite all of my ambitious plans and good intentions, really done almost nothing. My family had given me up as a failure. To make matters worse, I was beginning to share their opinion.

Casting about among my various ambitions for one which would require, first of all, no expenditure of money (I was, as always, quite broke), and second, one which I could undertake and carry out myself, without depending either on the cooperation of agents, directors, and producers, or on the smile of that lady named Luck who, at

least in my regard, seemed quite unamused. Knowing
nothing at the time of the mysteries of publishing generally, or of the vagaries of editors specifically, it seemed to
me that a long-projected, and equally long-delayed novel
was the ideal project. I could hardly wait to begin. Begin
I did. And today, seven years later, the manuscript remains half-completed. I was forced to face the fact that I
was not equipped by background and temperament for
writing. I lacked the discipline necessary to sit for hours at
the typewriter, and the skill and patience to work and
rework the story. Nonetheless, I struggled mightily to
finish the book. Instead, my subconscious took the easy
and ego-protective way out, and I became ill of what
obviously was a psychogenic disorder. Successive doctors
treated the condition as gallstones, gastritis, ulcers, and
various other internal ailments. I suffered greatly, the body
being unable to distinguish between physical and psy-
chosomatic pain.

Finding little relief from the doctors I had consulted,
and still less from the fees I was being charged, I turned
wholeheartedly to metaphysics for a cure. Sickness, fortunately, can be an effective prod, forcing one to take
measures that he would not consider if he were well.
Along with a number of metaphysical books, I read, for
the first time, the Bible. I had shunned the book for years,
associating it with superstition, fanaticism, and do-
goodism. I was in for an amazing revelation. I found it to
be honest, candid, real, and extremely topical. Even more
surprising, I found the Bible to be full of accounts of
psychical happenings and stories about psychical phenomena—about prophets, prophecies, healings, clairvoyance,
etc.

By the end of 1962 I felt strong enough, both physically
and spiritually, to become involved in a new and exciting
venture. I had been performing satirical skits in a Greenwich Village nightclub called Upstairs at the Duplex for
several weeks when I discovered that the owners were
looking for a manager for the place. It seemed a great
opportunity, and William McCarthy and I offered ourselves as co-managers and hosts. To our surprise and
delight, we were hired. William was to take care of the
business end of it, and I was to handle the entertainment.

Besides performing and producing the shows, I wrote material for a number of satirical revues that we presented. Some of today's top names in show business—such as Woody Allen, Joan Rivers, and Lainie Kazan—got their start at the Upstairs.

Business boomed, and I began to make plans for the future. It seemed that, at last, I had found an outlet for my theatrical ambitions. Among those plans was one for the organization of a satirical repertory group.

During this period I was busy constantly and had no time to continue along the road of the psychic, upon which I had just barely entered when William and I took over the Upstairs. After almost two years, however—by early 1964—we began to realize that the club was, or had become, a dead-end road for both of us. It provided a comfortable living, and it had been challenging and fun while it was still new. But now the novelty of it had begun to pall. My repertory group had not panned out, since those who were good enough to qualify for it were also too good to want to be tied down to one job for a long period of time. We both had to decide whether this was what we wanted out of life: security, routine, and boredom. In the face of that alternative, we gave notice and soon thereafter departed.

A group of people who had seen my work at the club offered to put up the money for a production of my own to be presented off-Broadway. It seemed that I was on the verge, finally, of crashing the theater in a big way. Everyone concerned worked long and hard, and we put on a good show. But the critics' reaction was what one might describe, kindly, as mixed. One, the New York *Daily News*, it is true, called the show "the best revue in recent years." But another said it was the worst. The others registered opinions somewhere between those two extremes. In the wake of such a bewildering response, the show lingered through a few performances and then closed. It had run about three weeks. Enormous amounts of time, effort, and money had been thrown away uselessly. Actually, it was all worse than useless. I was stigmatized as a "loser"; and in the theater the label means death to a career. There was no employment of any kind available to me.

Under the strain of failure and unemployment, my health began to deteriorate and my psychogenic stomach ailment returned to plague me. It was months before I recovered completely. By the end of 1964, however, I was back in harness. I organized an act with one of the actresses from my off-Broadway venture, a lovely and talented Negro named Marguerite Davis. We did satirical comedy, and we worked quite well together. After a few nightclub engagements, however, it became clear that the public was not yet ready to accept an integrated duo, comic or otherwise. Regretfully we broke up the partnership and I took a job at one of the pavilions at the New York World's Fair.

Hope and ego having been shattered beyond immediate repair, I drifted from one thing to another for a while. Then, William McCarthy told me of an extremely gifted Chicago medium who would be in New York for two weeks. She was holding group psychic meetings, and McCarthy had been invited. He asked me to go along, but I declined the invitation. At that point I had decided that that phase of my life was over. I had derived, it seemed, no benefit from my psychic experiences, and I wanted no more of it. I was still too young to have learned that self-pity is simply one facet of self-destructiveness.

McCarthy, nonplussed, went alone to the meeting. He reported to me afterward that it had been extremely interesting, and he insisted that I accompany him to the next one. Finally, to avoid arguing the point any further, I agreed.

The next meeting was held in the Fifty-seventh Street studio of artist Wayne Terry. The visiting medium was Deon Frey, a woman in her thirties. About ten people, including William McCarthy and me, were present.

Miss Frey is what is known as a "trance medium"; that is, she operates only while in a state of trance. In this instance, she prepared herself for the trance by a few moments of preliminary meditation. Then, her body became rigid and, when she began to speak, her voice had a harsh, almost masculine sound to it. Addressing each of us separately, she made a number of predictions, and she also made a few statements—quite accurate ones, apparently, to judge by the reactions of the people to whom they were addressed—about the past lives of several of the individuals present. Next, we were each allowed to ask one question of Miss Frey.

I asked, "What am I to do now?" I was careful to offer no clue as to my present situation or state of mind.

"Before this month is ended," came the reply, "you will have seen a completely new path on which to travel. It will be a kind of life entirely different from that which you are now leading. The present time is the right time for you. Do not be impatient. You will be guided."

There was a short pause. Then the voice continued. "It was a wise decision you made in not marrying Jo Ann. Your relationship, under the circumstances, could have ended only in complete disaster."

For a moment, the meaning of that ominous statement eluded me. Who was Jo Ann? But before I had had the time to puzzle it out, the voice cut in:

"No, not Jo Ann. I meant to say Johanna."

It struck me like a lightning bolt. About eight years before, I had been dating a singer named Johanna Kelly. We were very much in love, and talked of marriage; but, in the end, we decided that there were emotional problems involved that we could not work out, and we stopped seeing one another. No one in the room other than myself—not even my friend, McCarthy—knew anything about Johanna. It was a sore spot, seldom thought about and never spoken of.

After Miss Frey's trance was ended, I asked her if she could tell me anything about this message concerning Johanna—how it had come to her. She replied quite frankly that she could not, that she very seldom remembered after waking what she had said while in a trance.

It must have been obvious to the medium that I had been impressed by her performance, and when I told her about my own psychic experiences she seemed very interested.

"I am not unaware of your psychic ability," she said. "But I believe that, if someone has a gift, he should use it to full advantage."

"But that's exactly the problem," I answered. "I don't know how to do anything with it—or what to do even if I did know how. And I don't really understand very well what it is all about. In fact, I should tell you I don't believe at all that 'spirit entities' enter the medium's body and give those messages."

"All right. But where do you think the messages come from?"

"I don't know," was the feeble but candid reply. "And that may be one of the main reasons why I haven't gotten more deeply interested or involved in any of this. Perhaps I'm afraid of what I will discover."

Miss Frey was quick to reassure me on that score. "I've been giving seances for years," she said, "and I've been in innumerable trances. It's quite mystifying to me, too. But, despite all of the mystery, I have never seen or heard of one thing of which one could reasonably be afraid."

We continued talking in the same vein for a while. Before I left, Miss Frey had invited me to attend a seance she was giving the following week. "A group of Presbyterian and Episcopal ministers are interested in the investigation of life after death, and they have asked me to hold a trance session. It will be at the home of one of the ministers. If you'd like to come along with me, I'm sure it would be all right with them."

On the basis of what I had seen that night, I accepted. I must confess that, as strong as was my faith in Deon's gift, an added inducement was the thought of the orthodox (and therefore conservative) clergy being interested in the realm of the psychic. Even so, Deon's talent would have been sufficient incentive to attend other seances. There is at present a good deal of scientific investigation being done of parapsychological, or psychic, phenomena, and there is of course endless discussion and intellectualizing. But, with all due respect to the efforts of the scientists and to the good will of the people involved, it must be said that nothing can possibly be so convincing and worthwhile as evidence as one correct pronouncement made by a psychic to a person who is not expecting it. And Miss Frey's remarks about Johanna concerned an event of a very private nature that had taken place eight years previously. It seemed to me truly fantastic—too fantastic to be guesswork, or coincidence, or conjecture.

On the appointed day, Miss Frey—Deon, by this time— and I, along with another friend, Lisa Gladstone, arrived

at the Riverside Drive apartment of the Presbyterian minister who was to be our host. We were greeted at the door
by the minister's wife, a quietly charming lady who took
our coats and directed us to chairs in the living room. She
did not explain why the apartment was in total darkness,
and we were too shy to ask, so we stumbled to our places
in a state of some puzzlement. As my eyes became accustomed to the darkness, I was able to make out the forms
of approximately twenty people.

I had, as I said, seen Deon in trance before that
evening, and I have seen her many times since. But never
had she been so impressive as that evening, before those
reverend gentlemen and their ladies. She spoke in the
same voice that I had heard her use the week before,
giving the names of deceased relatives which the ministers
acknowledged to be correct. She then recounted incidents
and events in the lives of the men and women in the
room, going from one listener to the next without pause.
Even more astonishing than Deon's performance and the
accuracy of her observations was the attitude of unfeigned
interest and, certainly, of total lack of prejudice on the
part of the clergymen present as they conducted their
investigation. There was not a single witch-hunter among
them.

Deon did not forget her two escorts. She spoke first to
Lisa, advising her on an employment problem that she
was struggling with at that time. Then it was my turn.
"Marilyn, Marilyn," Deon's harsh voice whispered. "Marilyn's death was not intentional. It was a mistake. She
wanted to escape only for a time, but she took too many."

"Marilyn? And what is her last name?" I inquired,
somewhat timorously.

"Monroe," came the answer.

I should digress for a moment and explain that I have
always been an admirer of the late Miss Monroe—not of
the tawdry sex-goddess created by Hollywood in its own
image, but of the lovely, fragile, and unhappy person
beneath the glittering exterior. I had come into contact
with Miss Monroe only twice, once at a world première
when, for no apparent reason, she singled me out of a
crowd and kissed me on the cheek. The second time had
been at a party held for the benefit of the Actors Fund. I

saw, at this party, a deeply sensitive and complex human being, and I had wanted to speak with her at length, but I could not bring myself to impose upon someone who seemed not only lonely, but terribly shy.

In the days when I was writing satire for the stage, many of my skits concerned Marilyn Monroe. When I heard the news of her death, I was as shocked and saddened as though I had lost a close friend, for I felt as though I knew her personally and well. For months after her death, I would find myself thinking about Miss Monroe at odd moments, for no obvious reason. The night of Deon's trance, her name had come to me, quite vividly, the instant before Deon mentioned her. It was uncanny. Miss Frey was in New York for the first time. She knew me hardly at all—not even that I had been in show business. It was impossible that she could have discovered by the usual—i.e., nonpsychic—means that I had any particular interest in Miss Monroe.

Deon did not dwell on the subject of Marilyn Monroe. She passed on quickly to the next person in the room, and continued until she had made the complete circle. When the seance was over, we were thanked for coming, Deon was paid discreetly, our coats were handed to us, and we were led out into the hallway—all of which took place in the complete darkness in which we had spent the entire evening. I learned later that, in seances of this kind, darkness serves to protect the identities of those who attend. It is a useful expedient in that it allows some people to assist in anonymity who would be embarrassed if their presence were known to everyone in attendance. In this instance, I could only conclude that these ministers were committing an act tantamount to religious treason—consorting with the enemy, as it were. Hence, the need for the protection of darkness.

I attended other of Deon's seances while she was in New York, but she never again alluded to Marilyn Monroe's death. I could not, however, remove from my mind the episode during the ministers' seance. I went over it carefully in every detail, trying to uncover a purely natural explanation of how Deon could possibly have known of my feelings for the star. But there was no purely natural explanation.

One of Deon's subsequent seances was held in Wayne Terry's studio again, and the same people were present as at the first seance that I had attended. The purpose of this meeting was to test one of Deon's pet theories: that everyone is psychic to some extent, and that this psychic potential is able to be developed by the individual. For this purpose, Deon announced that we were going to have an evening devoted to psychometry. Psychometry—literally, "soul-measure"—is the receiving of impressions about individuals by holding in one's hand such small objects as rings and watches that they have had in their possession. The theory of psychometry is based on the belief that everything that has ever existed since the beginning of time has left a trace of its being in existence—not only in space or "ether," but on tangible objects, also, such as jewelry, books, clothing, etc. The person who holds a ring for a few moments, for example, is supposed to be able to sense sufficient data concerning the owner to enable him to tell something of that owner's past, personality, and so forth. It is, in my experience, the simplest of all psychic experiments, and it is made even more interesting by the fact that, in any given group, an unusually large number of people will respond with a high degree of accuracy. Even when played as a parlor game—as it frequently is—psychometry can have startling results.

Deon's psychometry meeting proved to be very successful. Each person was asked to contribute a personal object, which was then placed in a bowl. The objects thus collected were distributed among us. I was handed a set of keys. The entire operation was conducted in darkness, so that no one could know who put what into the bowl. After the distribution of objects, candles were lighted.

One by one, the participants began "sensing" things about the person whose contribution they held. A few of the group were amazingly adept at this, and were able to go into great detail concerning the subject's life, his ambitions, etc.

Holding the keys in my palm and listening to the others speak, I began to feel relaxed and drowsy. From where I was sitting, the most visible object in the room was a wavering candle flame, and I unconsciously fixed my eyes on that. Shortly, I felt myself drifting from my surroundings. I experienced a curious sensation of floating, and I seemed to be getting further and further away from the group and from Deon. Yet, I was not asleep; I was fully conscious of what I was experiencing and of what was going on around me.

In a moment I heard Deon say, "I think Daniel is going into a trance." Coming over to me, she spoke gently: "There is nothing to be afraid of, Daniel. You're going into a trance. But nothing bad or harmful will happen to you. I'll be here to guide you out of it. Now, open your senses. Allow the higher forces to take over. Let go, Daniel."

At first, I fought. I was frightened. I remembered too well the near-catastrophic experience when I first attempted the trance state. But, eventually, under the spell of Deon's soothing words, I had a feeling of confidence that all would be well, and I let go—that is, I relaxed, and stopped fighting. I felt now as though my real self were no longer in my body, but that I was floating above the group, looking down on them and on my body below.

Silence fell upon the room. No one spoke or moved. I began to twist and turn in my chair. My breathing became heavy. Low, indistinct sounds, mumblings, began to come from my mouth. Then a voice—an old, tired, querulous, and despairing voice, wholly unlike my own—spoke through my mouth: "Bill! Bill! Where are you?"

William McCarthy was present and, thinking that the voice was addressing him, he answered, "Yes. I'm here."

"Son of a bitch!" the voice rasped. "You're not Bill. Where's Bill?"

Deon stood up. "I know what this is. It has to do with my fiancé, Bill. His mother always used that expression, and that's her voice."

The voice interrupted Deon. "Bill—I can't let go of him. I don't want to, and I won't. I want him here with me. It's dark here. I must find Bill."

"Mother," Deon said, "Bill is not here. You've got to let him go now. You can't have him with you."

"I won't let him go, and I don't have to. You want him for yourself, but I'll be damned if you're going to have him. I'm going to take him, and I'll do it tonight!"

"Mother," Deon said firmly, "there is no reason for you

to take Bill. He is happy here. Please leave him alone. You'll lose his love if you continue like this."

"But I'm so lonely," Mother wailed. "There isn't anyone here."

"You haven't accepted the light. I told you this would happen, and you refused to listen while you were alive. You'll be alone forever if you don't turn toward the light." Deon's tone was severe.

"I can't walk," the voice continued. "It's just the same as before. Nothing has changed. This damned pain—my arms and hands hurt terribly."

(During the trance, while Bill's mother's voice was speaking through me, my body seemed to shrink to half its usual size, and my hands took on a crippled, almost clawlike appearance.)

"And who are all these people?" the voice demanded. "I don't know them. And they hate me!"

Everyone present protested that that was not so, that they wanted to help, not hurt. Johnny Lee Macfadden, widow of the famous health enthusiast, Bernarr Macfadden, rose from her place and crossed over to my chair.

"We all want to help you," Mrs. Macfadden said, resting her hand on my shoulder. "Won't you please turn away from darkness? You *can* walk, you know. The pain and suffering does not have to continue over there. Release yourself from that phase of your existence. Release Bill. Don't hold on to anything on the earthly plane. If you accept this, you'll be free of the pain and loneliness you suffered here and are continuing to suffer there."

The voice became weak. "But I can't walk. I can't see the light. And I'm so alone."

Mrs. Macfadden took my right arm and motioned Deon to take the left. Together, they lifted my body from the chair, but, being dead weight, it fell back. Again they tried, and this time they were able to aid me in walking slowly around the room. At first, my gait was spastic and faltering, but, as assistance was given, it became steady firm. The voice expressed thanks and said that it would try to release itself from the plane of earth and turn toward the light. After a while, it became unintelligible, then inaudible, and ceased altogether.

Deon immediately guided me out of the trance, assuring

me that everything was all right and telling me that I was coming out of it, that I was awakening. I had the feeling of floating down from the ceiling and back into my body, but I was not sure whether or not the whole thing had been a dream. The group assured me that it had not been.

Everyone, myself included, was eager to know the meaning of what had just taken place. Deon clarified the situation by explaining that she had a fiancé named Bill in Chicago. Bill's mother had been bedridden for an entire year before passing away. Earlier in life, she had been a devoutly religious woman, but a horribly painful and incapacitating arthritic condition had rendered her bitterly antireligious. Unable to walk, she lingered on, mostly with the strength of her will not to leave her son. She finally died, resentful, hating and bitter to the end.

Since his mother's death, Bill had had a most difficult time. Apparitions and dreams about his mother made his life, both waking and asleep, a continuing nightmare. In fact, the day after the seance, Deon spoke to Bill by telephone, and he described to her a particularly horrible dream that he had had the night before—i.e., the night of the seance.

A week later, the group met again. Eager to continue my exploration of this bizarre world, I went into trance once more. And once more the ancient, wavering voice spoke; but this time it had a tranquil, relaxed quality. First, it thanked the group for helping. Then it continued, "I am trying to turn toward the light. I will leave Bill alone. I will release him." And then it spoke no more.

Subsequently the apparitions and nightmares that had plagued Bill for so long became less frequent and finally ceased altogether.

In this whole mysterious occurrence, I had been functioning as a medium, in the literal sense of the word, in the classic form of the Spiritualistic seance. Yet, I was not completely convinced that the spirit, or soul—or whatever one wishes to call it—of Bill's mother had indeed entered my body. I could not argue, however, with the fact that the vocal, mental, and even physical characteristics that I had manifested during the trance were (as Deon assured me) incontrovertibly those of Bill's mother. In the face of this dilemma, I could only suspend judgment and hope that the future would resolve my doubts and clarify my understanding.

5

Those first trances at Deon's meetings were so dramatic and so successful that news of them spread quickly through New York City's large, but tightly knit, Spiritualist community. Several Spiritualist organizations contacted me upon learning of my abilities and asked that I speak for their groups. With Deon's encouragement, I decided to embark upon a career based upon my psychic talents. It was a decision I made rather quickly, and I had two major reasons for entering this new field as a professional. First, I was determined to satisfy myself with respect to a question that has always been of great importance to me, i.e., whether or not we survive in some form after death. Of course, I was also more than a little curious to find out what it was that had enabled me to function as I had during the trance sessions described. The second reason, to be perfectly candid, was that a career as a psychic seemed the only immediate way open for me to make a living, and perhaps even to achieve the success that had, up to then, always eluded me.

For the next two years—during 1964 and 1965—my psychic abilities were developed through the means afforded by organized Spiritualism. It was on the platforms of various Spiritualist churches and of related societies that I began demonstrating my psychic gift and lecturing about it. I should herewith point out, however, that I do not think of myself as a Spiritualist (even though I became an ordained minister in a Spiritualist organization for a short time, which is something I do not wish to go into now, for I have no desire of hurting any one person or

organization. As I mentioned earlier, if one works under
the guise of a Spiritualist group he is less likely to be
harassed by the police. The organization took me in and
ordained me, having seen my potential as a psychic.
Later, for many reasons, I bowed out of the organization).
But my early experiences in this field did stem from direct
contact with the Spiritualist movement.

Deon Frey, for example, is a Spiritualist, and it was
with her encouragement that I have become a career
psychic. And the reason that I did not completely go
along with the Spiritualist groups to any great length is
that my association with organized Spiritualism led me to
the conclusion that certain aspects of this religious movement have done much to retard, and actually to impede,
the progress of psychic investigation in the United States.

There are two reasons for this sad, and even paradox-
ical, situation. First, we should remember that, as Americans, we are not really very far removed, either in time or
in mentality, from the infamous witch-hunt hysteria of old
New England. The conjuring up of ghosts, spirits, and the
like, played a major role in that hideous episode, and, to
many people, there is still a residue of fear, mistrust, and
evil associated with anything as "different" and mysterious
as the occult. The word Spiritualism, therefore, because of
this heritage (and because of a good deal of fun-poking in
movies, books, television, etc.), is tainted by a connection
with, at best, fraud, and, at worst, with black magic and
voodoo and other forms of ritualistic nonsense. And I use
the word "nonsense" with more than a slight amount of
care. Having dealt with individuals who were harmed in
one way or another by "black magic," I cannot disregard
or dismiss it out of hand. I have noted, however, that
black magic never harms anyone who does not believe
that it *can* harm him. It is "sympathetic magic" in its most
malignant form; the mind of the person to be harmed,
working in consonance with the "witch" and believing that
it can and will be harmed, actually harms itself. "As a
man thinketh, so eventually he becometh."

The second reason is more concrete: Spiritualism is rife
with fraud. And this is so because the methods of Spiritualism are archaic, anarchic, and open to fakery. Persons
inclined toward Spiritualism make use of, and place their

trust in, those very things that make it possible for an unscrupulous "medium" to hoodwink them: ouija boards, crystal balls, cards, and other props. If the medium were truly psychic, he would not have to make use of anything material. It is a workable rule of thumb that most fake mediums deal with props of some kind.

An excellent illustration of this connection between props and fraud is the famous "trumpet seance," where the so-called souls of the dead are attracted by the presiding medium and speak to specific individuals in a darkened room through a trumpet which floats, illuminated, above the heads of those present. (The trumpet symbol is Biblical in origin; see, e.g., Rev. I, 10.) I, for one, have never been able to understand why the spirits of my loved ones would need anything as mundane as a trumpet to speak with me—particularly since they never used a trumpet while they were alive.

On the basis of my skepticism about trumpet-speaking spirits, I have seen many phony mediums during trumpet sessions. At one meeting, I grabbed the trumpet from the air as it bounced about over the heads of the assembled group. I discovered that the trumpet was held aloft by a very human hand, and I held on stubbornly—until I was slapped in the face by a second, equally human hand. I then crawled along the floor to the place where the medium had been sitting and found, without surprise, that the chair was unoccupied. I sat in it and waited. As the session was ending, the medium, no doubt tired of using different voices and juggling that trumpet, came back to his chair and sat squarely on my lap. I could sense his shock as he jumped forward and up. My point proved, I slipped back to my own chair. The lights were turned on, and I pretended to be very much absorbed by and impressed with the "phenomena" of the evening. The medium looked very uneasy the rest of the meeting. He is probably still trying to figure out who was sitting in his chair.

On another occasion, the president of a well-known and respected spiritual organization in New York sponsored a trumpet seance. The guest medium was one of the best-known trumpet mediums in the country, and he had been invited to demonstrate his gift in a meeting room at

Steinway Hall. The room had been rented from eight to
ten in the evening, and about twenty-five people had paid
a large fee to attend. Throughout the evening, the room
resounded with countless voices calling to those present,
giving names of departed loved ones, and communicating
"messages." It was quite impressive. The trumpet, glowing
mysteriously, had hovered eerily over the head of each
one in the gathering, and the voices were properly "spiritual" though loud and clear.

The session, however, had started late and ran over the
allotted rental period. A janitor, peeking into the darkened
room, thought that the meeting was over and that the
people had gone home. Whereupon, he flicked on the
lights—to disclose the medium poised in front of a member
of the group with his mouth to the trumpet, and his
assistant standing behind another chair and creating the
"waves of cold air" that the voices had said would accompany their presence.

The pseudo-medium got off easily. The people merely
demanded, and received, their entrance fees back.

Fakery is not an isolated phenomenon in the world of
the Spiritualist. It is organized, and even almost condoned
by certain powers-that-be of the Church. When I began
lecturing and giving psychic messages in the Spiritualist
churches, those in the hierarchy gave me many opportunities for advancement, and some of those opportunities
involved the use of deception. One afternoon, a well-
known and respected Spiritualist minister called upon me.
After a brief and inconsequential prologue, he said, "Daniel, we're proud of you in the movement. You're going
ahead rapidly and I wish to help you, to lighten your
burden. Most people interested in the occult sciences go to
different mediums, to different churches and lecture halls
to receive confirmation that life does exist in the hereafter
and to receive messages from their departed loved ones."

I wondered what all of this was leading up to. The
reverend minister did not keep me in suspense very long.

"Daniel, I know you have a divine gift. But remember
that no one is expected to work miracles. I think you
should make it easy on yourself. To help you do that, I
want you to look at a notebook I have with me. It can be
of importance to you. Many mediums use it. In it you'll

find the names of hundreds of people who regularly have readings or consultations with your fellow mediums. Next to each name is a list of relatives who have passed away and, possibly, some significant information about the individual consulting you, such as a recurring problem he has. This information was originally obtained by psychic methods and then put into the book. Your work will be a lot easier, and you can still say, quite truthfully, that all the information you give is of psychic origin. Remember that nothing convinces people of a gift in this field more quickly than being told the name of a dead loved one. It's truly a wonderful book. It contains the names of people from Maine to Florida, and you'll be amazed at how many of the people listed will come to you for consultations. They all seek out the upcoming, gifted newcomers."

He had just enough time to quote the asking price of the book—somewhere around three hundred dollars, I believe—before I ushered him bodily through the door. Since that time, and because of it, I rarely divulge any names that I may receive psychically to people who come for private consultations. Besides, names mean nothing. If a medium assured me that he could conjure up a dead relative and then told me that my Aunt Harriet was in the room, I'd expect Aunt Harriet to have something of value to tell me. Her name simply is not enough.

Another bit of psychic skulduggery is the routine of the "blindfolded billet reader." The blindfolded billet reader is a person who supposedly demonstrates psychic ability by placing two wide bands of tape over each eye in a cross design. Over the tape, he ties a thick scarf. In full view of the audience, the billet reader, with great ceremony, calls up a few people to inspect the tape and scarf and ascertain that he cannot see.

When the audience entered the meeting place, they had each written on a piece of paper their own names and two questions they wished the medium to answer, and then the names of two or three loved ones in the Spirit World. (These pieces of paper are not destroyed after the service, and I assume that this is one method of acquiring the information that goes into the aforementioned fraudulent notebook.)

The billet reader, taped and blindfolded, is handed the

basket in which the collected pieces of paper have been gathered. He stands on the rostrum and chooses a paper at random. Holding it to his forehead (which is symbolic, in occultism, of the third, or mystic, eye) he is able to give the name of the person and to answer the questions— supposedly using only his psychic sense.

In June 1965 I was asked to assist a world-famous billet reader during his performance at one of New York's Spiritualist churches. The reader was to perform first, and then, when he had tired, I was to step in and give psychic impressions to people in the audience. In this way, even those whom the reader had not had the time to answer would derive some benefit from the service, since I was told to concentrate on those individuals.

The billet reader was introduced, got up from his chair, and stepped to the rostrum. He taped his eyes in the usual manner and tied a scarf securely around his head. After he had been properly inspected, the basket of billets was placed on the rostrum and the billet reader began his performance.

I was seated on the dais, about four feet behind the reader. From that vantage point, it soon became apparent that he was a fraud. There was a reading lamp attached to the top of the rostrum from which the medium was operating, and it was that lamp that first aroused my suspicions. The glare from it shone directly and *glaringly* into my eyes, and, irritated and distracted by it, I could not understand why so strong a light—or any light at all, for that matter—was necessary. I watched the reader closely as he took several papers from the basket and placed them on the slanted top of the rostrum. Picking one from the pile, he held it to his forehead and began his demonstration. The audience, however, because of the podium's slanted top, could not see the reader's other hand, which held a second billet. The second billet was being turned over and over under the light. At first I thought that this was merely a nervous gesture, but then I noticed that, once the second billet was in a certain position, it was held under the light in a reading position. This happened several times. Finally, I could control neither my curiosity nor my suspicions any longer, and I moved my chair very quietly forward until I was barely two feet from the reader's left side. Watching his hidden hand, I saw that, in each case, the "nervous gesture" of turning the billet continued only until the writing on the paper was right side up.

Moving again, I watched the medium from directly under his left cheek, and in an instant the entire method of his fakery was clear. Where the two pieces of tape crossed over his eyes, they formed a corner just below the bridge of his nose. It was, in effect, an opening through which he could see. And the tape itself held the scarf away from the opening. This was, of course, impossible to detect from the front, where the audience was seated. But from my advantageous, if awkward, position it was painfully obvious. One last point puzzled me briefly. Some of the billets were inspected under the light, and then put aside and disregarded. Were the questions too difficult to answer? Not a bit of it. As it turned out, each of the rejected papers was written illegibly and too much time would have been spent deciphering it—with too much chance of error. It was to soothe the feelings of those who wrote illegibly that I had been engaged. I finished my part of the performance, left the church, and never returned.

It is difficult, even at the risk of seeming self-righteous, to have much sympathy with such a deliberate hoax as this. People usually come to psychics in time of great need, to find comfort and guidance. How anyone can be so heartless as to deliberately dupe them is beyond understanding. I have seen lives ruined by mediums who were either conscious fakes or who misused a true gift. The newspapers recount many instances of people who have been preyed upon; but the truth of the matter is that only a small fraction of the stories ever are made public. People who have been "taken" are usually afraid of the ensuing publicity and seldom report their losses. The following are but two of the numerous cases I have dealt with, which perhaps will serve to illustrate what happens to those who are not careful as to where they go in search of psychic counsel.

One lady had fallen in love with her surgeon after an operation. She went to a Spiritualist medium for advice. The medium apparently was quick to size up both the situation and the lady, and he took the easy way out in telling her what she obviously wanted to hear. "You are soul mates," he said, "made and destined for one another. You must pursue this man."

The smitten lady was, of course, delighted with this advice. She began a campaign of pursuit, which included innumerable telephone calls to the hapless surgeon and a deluge of letters. The poor man patiently explained to the woman that he was a happily married man, and that he could not return her feelings or respond to them.

The woman, puzzled by this reaction, returned to the medium. "Ah," he explained, "but this is really a very unhappy marriage. His wife is an evil woman, and she is working to destroy this man. You alone can save him, and you must do so in spite of his apparent unwillingness." He corroborated his position by telling her also that she and the surgeon had been together in a previous life, that they had accidentally been separated in a process of reincarnation, and that they must come together again at any cost.

The woman was convinced, and determined. She went to the doctor's office and, when he refused to see her, sat there all day. She repeated this tactic for several days. Finally, the doctor called in the police and had the woman removed by force when she began creating emotional scenes in his waiting room. She was taken to Bellevue Hospital's psychiatric observation ward, where it was established that she was, after all, legally quite sane. After her release, the woman came to me for help.

Before she could make herself comfortable in my living room I sensed what her problem was, and told her immediately that she was in serious trouble. "You have been the victim of a cruel hoax," I said. "If it continues, you will be hurt even more than you have already been."

The lady was very disturbed by my analysis of her situation, and perhaps by my bluntness. Nevertheless, she quietly told me the entire story, from beginning to end, and then waited for my reaction. Again, I told her that she had been taken in by a phony medium, and that there was not the slightest chance that anything could be worked out between herself and the surgeon. And I advised her immediately to forget all about him and to develop some other interest in life.

This, obviously, was not what the lady wanted to hear. She had come to me with the hope that I would confirm her medium's story and thus furnish her with fresh ammunition for the pursuit. She thanked me for my time and advice and left. I never saw her again, but I feel that she may have gotten into further difficulty as she was quite determined to be with this man and not to be put off by any such consideration as the trouble she might cause for him, or the embarrassment that might result for her. The unscrupulous medium had done his work well.

Another case involved a wealthy and socially prominent New York matron. The lady had been interested in the occult since childhood and had delved into Spiritualism. Her masseuse, apparently knowing a good thing when she saw it, confided to the lady one day that she was also a medium, and that she used the ouija board in her work.

The lady had already confided to the masseuse-medium that she wanted to give financial help to an invalid nephew, but that she was hesitating because she did not know whether the child's parents would resent her interference in their affairs. Now the masseuse suggested, "Let's ask the ouija board." They did, and the ouija board spelled out Y-E-S; and then, in full sentences, it told the lady not only that she should indeed help the child, but also that it was her obligation to do so.

When asked whose spirit was working the board, the ouija board spelled out F-A-T-H-E-R. Moreover, in answering the questions asked by the lady, the board used certain phrases and words that her father had often employed. The con game was on.

As time passed and the plot thickened, the board recommended that the lady discharge her old lawyer and engage a new one. Predictably, the lawyer suggested by the board happened also to be the masseuse's attorney. The matron went to her new attorney's office to establish a one-hundred-thousand-dollar trust fund for her nephew. With incredible naïveté, she turned over the money to the attorney, and he told her that it would be a few weeks before the papers were ready for her signature. Actually, he put her off for months without either returning the money to her or showing any signs of establishing a trust fund. The truth of the matter was that he had diverted the money to his own use.

In the meantime, the masseuse, not to be outdone by her accomplice, had also talked the lady into giving her large sums to pay various "mystics" for healing work that they would perform for the invalid child. Then, probably to prevent any interference in her schemes, the masseuse, with the help of her ouija board, managed to alienate the lady from her family by telling her that the family was ashamed of the child and that they were angry because of the help she was attempting to give. The lady confronted her family with this information, and they, perhaps understandably, concluded that she had lost her reason. They instituted legal proceedings to deprive her of the trusteeship she exercised over her father's estate, and it was only after a lengthy and financially depleting court battle that her legal sanity was established.

The matron is an intelligent, well-educated woman. Ordinarily she would never have become the victim of such a crude and time-worn con game, but she was more or less at the mercy of circumstances, since she felt compelled to help her nephew and the ouija board confirmed her in the line of action that she felt to be right. The "clincher," of course, was her belief that her beloved father's spirit was operating the board.

The lady first came to me about the lawyer, whose procrastinations and machinations in regard to the trust fund had aroused her suspicions. During my first meeting with her, I named the masseuse-medium as the one who basically was the cause of her predicament. At first, she would not believe this of one whom she considered her friend; but, as time went on, I was able to explain to her just how she had been bilked.

Eventually, many of this lady's problems were able to be solved. She was reconciled with her family; the lawyer went to jail for fraud; and the medium-masseuse is, at this moment, awaiting trial on a similar charge. All in all, it was a sordid business, and it required many months of psychic guidance to help straighten out this unfortunate lady's situation.

These instances are not recorded here because of their sensational aspects, but rather in order to put the reader on guard. Even if one loses only a few dollars to a fake medium, one is still being taken. And I would say that at least seventy-five percent of the mediums that I have seen who deal in Spiritualism have proved, in one way or another, to be frauds and/or con men.

But what about the remaining twenty-five percent? These cannot be shrugged off as doing particularly lucky guesswork. My experiences, for example, in the Connecticut church, and those with Deon Frey and with other Spiritualists I have seen in action, cannot be dismissed lightly. One medium recently in the news*—in the New York *Times* of September 27, 1967—is Arthur Ford, a Spiritualist, who has been examined and observed in his work by eminent scientists. These latter report that the messages that Mr. Ford claims to receive from the spirit world can only be described as being, somehow, authentic.

*Re the famous seance with Bishop Pike.

Because of the proof that I have received from these few honest and gifted mediums, and because of the nature of the work that I myself have become involved in, I have been forced logically to come to some conclusion concerning the source of these messages. It is this—and the reader is free to accept or reject it as he sees fit: I believe that something of the soul, or subconscious mind, or psyche (or whatever one wishes to call it) does survive after death in some form. In some unknown way, our thinking processes continue. True psychics are able to receive impressions from these processes—or, if not from them directly, then about them from those they have left behind. Like a good receiver in modern television equipment, a medium is able to pick up or read the ever-recurring psychic vibrations from the past, present, and future. The principle is a sound scientific one: time, as the measure of change, is purely subjective; therefore, everything that has been, or will be, is.

6

During the first two years of my career as a professional psychic, I was never able fully to accept the fact that I had finally found my life's work. There was still a strong temptation to regard it as something temporary, something to support me until "something" turned up for me in my first love, the theater. I was at great pains to retain the friends, acquaintances, and "contacts" that I had in show business, and I harbored secret hopes of keeping one foot in the door—just in case. In fact, on many occasions, up until late 1966, I attempted to return to the theater. But I was frustrated each time. In need of income, and having received many requests to do so, I started a private consultation practice. In spite of myself, I still had the sensation of becoming more and more deeply involved in something that I really didn't want to be involved in at all.

To say that I "started a private consultation practice" sounds perhaps rather grand and formidable. Actually, the process was simplicity itself. There were a number of people who were in the habit of consulting me regularly on personal and business problems. I merely let them know that I was now "in business" on a full-time basis. Before long, the word spread among my friends and theirs, and I had as many clients as I could handle.

Since that time, I have gradually lost my desire to return to show business. The hundreds of readings I have given over the past three years have been for me an immensely rewarding experience. Working with individuals, helping them, and guiding them psychically has been far more satisfying and fulfilling, I am sure, than anything that I could have accomplished in the theater.

In giving these private consultations, I do not go into a

trance. Trance work is exhausting, and takes much preparation in most cases. Moreover, I have found that, in the vast majority of cases, a trance is not necessary for me to be able to function at optimum efficiency and accuracy. A consultation does, however, require some preparation. I must, for example, work to clear my mind of my own thinking, my own feelings. I must, as it were, subdue my own consciousness so as to leave my mind open to psychic impressions. Usually I accomplish this by a series of short meditations (which I will explain later in the book). At first, it was necessary for me to go through this process of preparation before each consultation. At present, however, I find that it is sufficient for me to do it once, at the beginning of the day; probably I am beginning to exercise conscious control over my mind and emotions.

During the course of a reading or consultation, I am not aware of any force, or Spirit. Psychic impressions come to me as thoughts; that is, they simply occur to me, out of the blue. I do not hear "voices," and I have never had an "apparition." The whole process seems to me quite natural and unforced, and in that respect my impressions differ from guesses or "hunches" in that these latter imply the conscious searching for a conclusion. The only effort involved is that of clearing my mind and "tuning in"—which is the preparation referred to above.

As one may gather from the above, I am pretty much myself during a reading, and I am perfectly conscious of everything going on around me—telephones ringing, doorbells, etc. The only distractions I am subject to are those that interfere with any normal, serious conversation, but even those are minor distractions for me since I do have to maintain a certain level of concentration on what I am doing. In case of an interruption during the reading—and I do my best to avoid such interruptions, more out of consideration for my client than from any difficulty that it creates in receiving impressions—I simply "turn off"; that is, I deliberately shut my mind to psychic impressions. This ability to turn on and turn off at will is a great blessing, not only because it is so convenient during consultations but also because it enables me to lead a normal social life, without "tuning in" inadvertently to any psychic emanations from my friends—which might be, in a sense, an invasion of their privacy.

It is my own estimate that my psychic impressions are accurate in eighty percent of the cases in which I give them. Frankly, I do not know how to account for the remaining twenty percent. I have my suspicions, of course—resistance, skepticism, or some sort of resistance, conscious or otherwise, on the part of the client, or a reluctance on his part to provide wholly accurate data for me to work from. It is likely that, with the passage of time, my degree of accuracy will improve. I suspect, however, that it is unlikely that it will ever approach anything like one hundred percent, because there are so many variables—i.e., human factors—involved. In the meantime, I am content with eighty percent accuracy, which seems to me, from my experience with other mediums, a rather high percentage.

It is not so much this high degree of accuracy, taken alone, which has been responsible for whatever success I have enjoyed on television, the radio, and the lecture platform, as it has been my ability to demonstrate this gift at any given time; that is, to turn on and off at will. Thus, I have been spared the embarrassment of "going dry" at a crucial moment. And it is this ability that has been a major factor in forming my belief that the mental and psychic functions of a person continue after death in some form, and that the psychic medium is simply one who is able to tune in to them. I am, therefore, a far distance from the orthodox Spiritualist credo concerning the existence of human-like souls or ghosts whom one may or may not contact, depending upon the disposition of the soul at the moment.

Logically, then, I do not believe in Heaven or Hell; but I believe that we create these states of mind ourselves here on earth and, after the transition called death, they continue, and are perceptible to the medium in the form of "vibrations" or emanations. A person who was wicked on earth, therefore, gives off the same waves after death, and a good man's emanations are, of course, good after death. And this also explains how, in the case of the mother of Deon Frey's fiancé, I received the hateful, selfish, and disgruntled vibrations of a person who, when alive, had been hateful, selfish, and disgruntled.

In short, I do not need to go into a trance or to contact a "spirit" in order to receive psychic impressions. I simply turn on and tune in to the vibrations around me, and I then receive the information that is necessary to help, advise, and guide the person who has come to me for a reading.

A reading or consultation typical of what I usually do was the one seen on television during 1967 under the title "Daniel Logan: a Man Who Predicts Your Future." The show, a "special," was produced by David Susskind as the result of widespread interest generated by my earlier appearance on his interview program. It was, as the title suggests, an in-depth study of me and my gift, and it consisted of a series of short psychic impressions for various members of the audience, a discussion with two eminent investigators of extrasensory perception, and an unrehearsed on-camera reading with a guest celebrity.

The most interesting part of the show, so far as I was concerned—and the part that best illustrates how I give a reading—was the interview with the guest celebrity, who in this case was actress Betsy von Furstenberg. At the point in the show where I gave Miss von Furstenberg the reading, the studio lights were lowered and the audience was asked to be absolutely quiet. We were attempting to simulate the atmosphere of a private consultation, such as we should have had if Miss von Furstenberg had come to my office.

It should be noted that I had not met Miss von Furstenberg before the filming of the show. I recalled seeing her on several television shows and reading about her in a social column or two, but nothing more. Even at the studio itself, I had not seen or spoken to her until she appeared before the cameras.

Now, sitting opposite her, I said, "There is a word that comes to me, color. There is a tremendous amount of color about you, and your favorite color is blue-green."

"That's true," she said—discreetly checking her apparel to see if there was any blue-green in sight. There wasn't.

"Color is a key word with you; for, although you are an

actress by profession, I feel that you work with your hands in a creative way, with colors. Do you paint?"

"Yes, I do. And only a few friends know that."

"In painting, you use a great deal of the blue-green that I mentioned. In fact, you tend to go overboard with it, and sometimes your colors are too vivid in the paintings. That is a criticism that has been made of your work."

"Yes, that's true."

"You should continue with your painting. At some time in the future, you will be even better known as an artist than you are as an actress. This will probably happen within the next eight to ten years."

Miss von Furstenberg looked interested—and delighted.

"There is also something musical about you," I continued. "You're studying singing, aren't you?"

"Yes, I am! And only my family and a few close friends know about that."

"That, too, is something you should continue with. I feel that you will be doing a musical comedy in the very near future. There is a contract for it before you. Musical comedy is a new phase of your career that you should enter now."

"I've always wanted to do a musical," she said.

(This show was taped in March of 1967. Miss von Furstenberg opened in a Broadway musical in May of 1967, and in a second one in the fall of 1967.)

"You have two children, a boy and a girl. Yet, somehow, I get the impression of three children—in fact, I almost said three. Did—did you lose a child? Did you have a miscarriage?"

"Yes, I did," was the shocked answer. "By miscarriage!" Despite the very personal turn that the reading had taken, this charming lady never once lost her composure. In fact, the more I told her, the more open and receptive she became. It was a remarkably easy reading.

"You seem to like Europe," I told her, "and I see that you spend much of your time there. I am receiving an impression—something about Switzerland, something about some property or a house there."

For a moment, Miss von Furstenberg looked almost uncomfortable. "Not Switzerland," she said. "It's in Rome."

After the show, Miss von Furstenberg told David Susskind that I had indeed been right, that there was something about land and a house in Switzerland, but that she could not, because of legal considerations, speak of it. Several times, unfortunately, I have hit upon something that the person being interviewed did not care to have disclosed publicly. Several times, too, I have been up against people who are determined that I am going to be wrong no matter what I say. One such instance occurred during my appearance on Mr. Susskind's television interview show, when one young lady from the audience denied three things that I had told her about herself. After the show, she came up to me and apologized, in Mr. Susskind's hearing. For no reason, she confessed, she had just wanted to embarrass me and "throw me off."

My reading with Miss von Furstenberg was particularly successful, apparently because I had been able to reveal things unknown to the public from the actress' past, her present, and her future. And I was very grateful that so many confidential images about her had come to me.

After that show, I received approximately fourteen thousand requests for readings, by way of letters, telegrams, telephone calls, and other means. Among those letters, there was one which particularly illustrates what I would like to believe is the significance of my readings. It read, in part:

Dear Mr. Logan:
   Your method of reading character, motive, and purpose impressed us deeply, as your approach is moral. To encourage the insecure, to strengthen those who are trying to do right, to check possible wrong moves, etc., this seems the proper way to use such gifts as yours.

This letter came from two sisters, Margaret and Ruth Geiger, who live on Long Island. They are both artists who had been permanently crippled in an accident some ten years before. Their letter was a request for guidance and asked specifically whether I felt that they would walk again, and what field of activity I thought they should become involved in. I answered, saying that I felt they would be able to walk again and that they must seek a cure "close at hand." Time and effort would be required for the cure, but it would surely come. I also said that they must continue the work in which they were then involved (art work with children), as this would see them through. I further advised them to write their story and submit it for publication as an inspirational article, for I felt that it would be bought and published by a major magazine.

Four months later, I received a reply to my letter: "Your kindness filled us with a wonder and great happiness. We were instantly transported to a land of hope, banishing dread. This urged us to continue a cure we first heard of a year ago, and it is already showing marked results with me, so that I am walking and doing quite a bit of heavy work. With your insight, you surely must feel the great lift we have received from your reading. We have spent the last few months writing our story and everyone finds it interesting. Of course, these are people, young and old, who know us and have seen us both helpless as well as improving to our present state. It was difficult writing the article, but your reading kept us at it; our thought was synthesized by the task. Our warm and earnest gratitude. (signed) Ruth Geiger." Letters such as this not only inspire me to continue with my work, but · they also serve to assure me that I have done the right thing in making a career of psychic consultation. I have since met the Geiger sisters. I have seen them rise from their wheelchairs and walk a few steps. I have read their story, and it is honest and touching. It is more rewarding than I could have imagined to know that I have been able to be of help to them, and to many people like them.

Such readings as that of the Geiger sisters are rather dramatic in nature, but, although it proved to be of value to them, it offers little to convince the skeptic who requires concrete proof of my gift. And skepticism is undoubtedly one of the great problems that I have to face every day of my working life. It is no exaggeration to say that I spend more time explaining and defending my gift than I do in actually putting it to use. Happily the situation seems to be on the mend. The door seems to be opening on the psychic world. Where fear, cynicism, and an unreasoning demand for total accuracy once almost ended scientific research in the field of extrasensory perception, we now see a new age dawning. Many major universities now offer at least lecture courses in the various manifestations of that phenomenon. One may hope that this new age will bring a time when the natural human psychic sense will be developed and put to use by coming generations.

In the meantime, all one can do is advance evidence of authentic psychic phenomena, in the hope of confirming the interest of those who are intrigued by this new and largely unexplored field and of disarming, insofar as this is possible, the skeptics.

For that purpose, I have gathered together excerpts from some of the more interesting readings that I have given.

1. *Viola Hooven*, Manhattan art collector and connoisseur. During a reading with this lady, I made some reference to a collection of statues that she had not mentioned, but that I had sensed psychically that she had.

"I don't know what you mean," was her first reaction.

"Don't you have a collection of very old, almost ancient statues in a room of your apartment?"

"Oh, that. Yes. You must mean my collection of pre-Columbian art."

"Well, I don't want to alarm you, but most of the pieces are not what they purport to be. In fact, most of them are fakes." The phrase "fake statues in another room" had come to me quite strongly.

"I'm sorry, but I really can't go along with that. The entire collection is worth about twenty thousand dollars, and I have the authentication papers for each piece."

"I'm sorry too, but I can't change what is. I'm quite sure that if you have them checked out, you'll discover that most of the statues are fakes."

Still doubting, but disturbed enough to want to discover whether or not she had indeed bought fake statues, Miss Hooven packed her treasures and, with my assistance, carted them to the office of the distinguished Curator of Pre-Columbian Art in New York's Museum of Natural History, Dr. Gordon Echolm. Dr. Echolm examined the pieces carefully one by one, and he put many of them to one side. These, he explained, were either not authentic at all, or had had so much restoration done to them that they could hardly be called authentic in the proper use of the term. He kept the collection for several weeks, and made a detailed list of what was and what was not authentic pre-Columbian art. Miss Hooven, on the basis of that list, is presently negotiating with the dealer from whom she bought these objects for the return of her money.

2. *Miss Nid Tongootai*, formerly of Thailand, presently owner of The Nid of Thailand Shop in New York City, importer of fine silks and fashion designer.

I went into Miss Tongootai's shop as a customer one day, and stayed for a lengthy conversation. When she learned what field I was in, she asked me whether I could tell her anything about herself.

"I see that you have property in Thailand," I answered, "and that you are trying to sell this land."

"Yes, that's right."

"You will sell it within the next three months."

"I hope you are right," Miss Tongootai answered, "but it's been on the market for a long time. It's hard to believe that I could sell it very soon, after having waited so long. Tell me, if I do sell it as you say, will I get the price that I am asking for it?"

"No, you won't," I told her, "but it will be very close—just a few thousand dollars less than what you are asking."

I learned from Miss Tongootai later that the property was indeed sold for one or two thousand dollars less than her asking price, almost exactly three months after our initial conversation. At that time, I also advised her to sell the rest of her property in Thailand, since I sensed that that country would soon become involved in the Vietnam war. A few days later, quite unexpectedly, it was announced that Thailand had sent its first troops to Vietnam.

A short time later, Miss Tongootai took charge of the Thailand Pavilion at the New York World's Fair. Unfortunately she shared the fate of the Fair in general in that she did not do nearly so well there as she had expected. With that experience behind her, she was hesitant about participating in Montreal's Expo '67, and she asked my advice on the matter.

"Yes," I answered immediately. "You should go, by all means. Expo '67 will be the most successful of all the Fairs, and, if you don't participate, you will regret it the rest of your life. Your only problem there will be that you won't have enough goods to sell because people will be buying from you at such a tremendous rate. So, please be sure to order extra large quantities of your merchandise before you leave for Canada."

Miss Tongootai did open a shop at the Montreal Fair, and the success of Expo '67 is, of course, a matter of history. Happily the demand for her goods was so great that she was constantly running short and having to order more from Thailand.

3. *Nadia Horowitz*, Manhattan artist.

I met Miss Horowitz at a social function and, at her request, gave her an impromptu reading even before I knew her name. I spoke of the recent death of someone whom she had loved very much. She acknowledged that her husband had died shortly before.

"The most important thing in your life is color," I told her. "You must be a painter. You have done something unusual and different with the paint itself—not with its color, but something else."

"Yes, that's right. I've developed, over a period of years, a certain kind of paint that has the look and texture of velvet."

"Your work, your paintings, are very difficult and abstract. But there is one that I can almost see. It has reds, yellows, and oranges, and contains a message of some kind, something having to do with the Bible. It is a beautiful work of art."

This was one of those rare instances where I actually saw an object quite clearly in my mind before viewing the material reality itself. The painting, when I did see it, turned out to be exactly as I had envisioned. There were many shades of yellow, orange, and red, and the painting represented Moses and his people in the desert.

4. *Miss Ulla Okensus*, formerly of Sweden, now of New York.

During a private reading I asked Miss Okensus if she

were not planning a trip back to her native Sweden. She replied affirmatively.

"I sense that your health has not been good lately. Is that not so?"

"You are correct," she answered. "But nevertheless I feel that I must go back to Sweden for a visit, just the same."

"Please don't be upset," I cautioned her, trying to soften the blow of information that I knew to be unpleasant, but necessary, "but you must be very careful. You have been feeling very depressed lately, and your depression is justified because it is being caused by a deterioration in your health. I must tell you that you will have to have an operation in a short time, and I'd strongly advise you to delay your trip to Sweden for a while. Otherwise, you will have to have the operation in Europe. Please try to have it taken care of before you leave."

"It's not that I don't believe you, and I'm grateful for your warning. But I simply must get to Sweden very shortly."

Miss Okensus did leave for Sweden as planned. Several months later I received a letter from her, telling me that, immediately upon arriving in Europe, she had been taken seriously ill and had to be rushed to the hospital, where an emergency operation was performed.

5. *Ariel Taylor*, famous Manhattan astrologist.

Miss Taylor came to me for a reading, during the course of which I foresaw a death in her immediate circle. Knowing how such news would affect the lady, I tried to soften the blow by speaking vaguely, without identifying the person whose death I felt was imminent. Miss Taylor, misinterpreting my well-intentioned, but perhaps clumsy, attempts at circumlocution, thought that it was her own death I foresaw and asked me, at the end of the reading, if I could tell her how long she had yet to live.

At that point, I saw that it was useless to try to withhold anything from Miss Taylor. "It was not you, but your husband, whose death I foresaw," I said. "Please try to face this and accept it. If you are not prepared, then you will yourself become seriously ill from the shock of his death."

Miss Taylor, quite understandably, was unwilling to accept the accuracy of my prediction. She protested that her husband, although he was elderly, was in very good health. Nonetheless, a few weeks later her husband fell and broke his hip. He never recovered, and died soon after.

6. *Barry Farber*, Manhattan radio star.

I was invited to appear on Mr. Farber's radio show, and during the course of the interview I asked him whether he knew anything about a television show that he would soon be connected with.

"No, I don't know anything about that," he said.

"Within the next year and a half," I continued, "you will be doing a television show which will be much like the one you are doing now on radio. I mean that it will be an interview show."

In the fall of 1967—almost exactly eighteen months later —Mr. Farber began a new television series called "What Is ——— Really Like?" It was an interview show designed to allow the audience to see what ———(a celebrity) really is like, and Mr. Farber was the host.

7. *Richard Lockman*, vice-president of Van Heusen Shirts, Manhattan.

I met Mr. Lockman at a social function, and we talked eventually about our respective occupations. Like a good, hardheaded businessman, Mr. Lockman was skeptical about anything as intangible as extrasensory perception and clairvoyance, and insisted on testing what I assured him was not magic but a true, practical gift. The field that he selected for the test seemed to me not only more mysterious and unpredictable than any form of occultism, but it was one in which I never have had the slightest interest: the stock market.

"I'll tell you the name of a stock that I own," he proposed, "and you tell me what's going to happen to it during the next few weeks."

Ordinarily I turn down this sort of request. For some reason, it seems vaguely immoral to predict the course of the market, just as it seems immoral to foresee the out-come of a horse race. In addition, there is always a chance that my prediction will be wrong, and a good deal of money will be lost through my fault. In this case, however, Mr. Lockman was so thoroughly convinced that I had no gift at all and that extrasensory perception was a lot of hokus-pokus, that I could not resist the temptation to prove him wrong. Besides, there seemed little likelihood that he would act on any advice that I gave him about the stock market.

"All right. What stock are you interested in?"

"Amphenol. What impression do you get of Amphenol?"

I had never even heard of Amphenol, and I didn't know whether it was a drug, or a cosmetic, or a gun. "What price did you originally pay per share for this stock?"

"About twenty-five and three-quarters per share," Mr. Lockman answered.

"And what exactly do you want to know about it?"

"I want to know how high it will go. And let me add, Mr. Logan, that no one, not even the best stockbroker in the world, can or would try to guess at what point a stock will reach its peak. If you can do it, it will be fantastic. Now, tell me, do you think that Amphenol will go up to fifty?"

"No, it won't go that high."

"How about forty?"

"Not that high, either."

"Thirty-five?"

"A little higher than that," I said.

"How much higher? Thirty-seven? Thirty-eight?"

"Thirty-eight. It will go up to thirty-eight, and then it will drop."

"All right. We'll see. I'll let you know how your guess worked out."

This exchange took place in late September 1967. A short time later, Mr. Lockman explained to me what had happened. It seems that he, like most people who invest quite a bit—particularly for short-term profits—had given his stockbroker the power to sell his stock when the broker felt that the proper moment had arrived; that is, when he felt that the stock had reached its peak. When Amphenol reached 31¾, or six points higher than when Mr. Lockman had bought it, the broker sold. This was on a

Wednesday, and Mr. Lockman did not know that the stock had been sold. Opening the newspapers the next day, he saw that the stock had gone up to 34 and a fraction. On Friday, when the stockmarket closed, he called his broker in order to check on his holdings. The broker told him that he had sold the Amphenol when it reached 31¾, and that he wished that he had waited, since it had gone higher.

"Yes," Mr. Lockman answered, "I know. I saw in the papers yesterday that it had gone to thirty-four."

"But that's only the half of it," the broker replied. "It climbed some more this afternoon. It went up to—"

Before the broker could finish, Mr. Lockman interrupted him. "I know, I know. Don't tell me. It went up to thirty-eight, didn't it? And then it went down. Is that correct?"

"Yes," the dumbfounded broker answered. "But how did you know that?"

"I'll tell you about it some day," Mr. Lockman said. "You won't believe it."

Mr. Lockman's attitude today is no longer one of total skepticism.

7

It has been only recently, as I said, that I have achieved a degree of contentment as a professional psychic. Before that, I was constantly being bitten by "the worm that never dieth"—in my case, show business. The need to express myself on the stage seemingly was impossible to subdue. Months of vacillating between my consultation practice and the theater, coupled with frustration in my attempts to get a role—any kind of role—brought on a state of severe depression. I decided to go on a vacation to Florida. It was a fairly uncomplicated project. I was living at the time in a house trailer just outside of New York City, and it was simply a matter of driving off with the trailer in tow.

On December 20, 1965, I started out—with a friend, Bill, and a (lady) cousin, and my two white cocker spaniels. In addition, the trailer—all thirty-five glistening feet of it—housed: seven African finches, a six-year-old tame English sparrow, and Shoogoondala, who is a formidable-looking, but quite docile tortoise. I have never outgrown my need to love and care for animals, and it is easier to take them on a trip with me than to attempt to find a temporary home for such a menagerie.

Our venture prospered through Pennsylvania, Virginia, and the Carolinas. But, as we neared the border of Georgia, I began to feel uneasy. I had told my companions before starting that under no circumstances were we to stop in that state. The reports of racial hatred and violence that had been received from Georgia filled me with abhorrence, and I wanted no part of this aspect of the "deep South."

As though echoing my misgivings, as we approached Georgia the highway became a twisting, turning, one-lane ordeal. Up to then, the trip had been very comfortable— we were driving my cousin's new Ford—and we had not even bothered to fasten our seat belts. Now, however, dusk was settling, and suddenly, from out of nowhere, I heard a voice saying clearly, "You'd better fasten your seat belts! You'd better fasten your seat belts!" My companions, both of whom were accustomed to the way in which my psychic sense worked, needed no urging once I had told them of the warning that I heard, and all three of us fastened our seat belts.

It was now dark, and as we rode, our eyes were fastened to the ever-curving pavement ahead of us. A fog-enveloped swamp lay on either side of the highway, and the mist drifted over the road, occasionally blocking it from view. Suddenly a dog darted out of the swamp and planted himself squarely in the middle of the road, directly in our path. The driver veered slightly to the left, hoping to miss the animal, but the trailer started swerving on its own and began pulling us from one side of the highway to the other. As it swerved, it gained tremendous momentum and swung around in front of the car with such force that we were snapped free of the trailer hitch, and the car turned over and over and landed in the swamp on the left side of the highway.

The next thing that I recall was finding myself on my hands and knees in a sea of shattered glass. Bill, who had been driving, still clutched the steering wheel while dangling upside down inside the car, and my cousin hung in a similar position on the other side of the seat. Their seat belts had held. The thought passed through my mind that comes very quickly and unexpected; one moment, we had been speeding through the night; the next, because of a circumstance completely beyond our control, the car lay smashed beyond recognition in a Georgia swamp.

We were told later by officials that, had it not been for the fact that our seat belts were secured, at least two of us almost certainly would not have survived the crash. The doors of the car were folded like accordions, the roof was crushed, the front wheels and the hood were demolished beyond repair. The gas tank, which we had filled only ninety minutes previously, by some miracle had not exploded.

From my kneeling position inside the car, I looked out from what had once been the windshield and saw the left front wheel spinning madly in space. Then the dogs, panic-stricken and hurt, scrambled out of the car and dashed back toward the highway. Slithering out of the shattered side window, I ran, grabbed them—and fell to the ground with an excruciating pain in my lower right back. The others also managed to get out of the wreck on their own power.

It was only a moment before the local police and the sheriff arrived. They had already radioed for ambulances, convinced that they would find us seriously injured, and perhaps dead. The sheriff helped us to his car and sped to the nearest hospital, which was in Hinesville, Georgia. I couldn't help recalling my last words before starting on the trip: "Remember. No matter what, we don't stop in hateful, segregated Georgia."

After a number of X-rays, the doctor at the hospital told Bill and me that we had fractured vertebrae. Bill also had two broken ribs. We would have to remain in the hospital for some weeks, and then spend two or three months wearing braces. My cousin, miraculously, was unhurt, except for a few bruises and scratches.

Naturally, to the end of my days I shall be grateful for the psychic warning that enabled us to protect ourselves at least to the extent of fastening our seat belts. But, once in the hospital, I could not help feeling a certain bitter resentment against the "voice." If we could be warned, then why couldn't we have been totally protected? Why did we have to go through the accident at all? I believed then, as I do now, that everything that happens to one is meant to teach one something; it happens in order to enable one to grow. But, at that time, I couldn't understand what I could possibly learn from being hospitalized in Georgia.

The lesson was not long in coming. What I feared would be an uncomfortable stay in a fear-gripped, hostile, intolerant state proved instead to be an eye-opener. First, the sheriff—the "small-town, Southern sheriff" who is nowadays the villain of so many popular pieces—drove my cousin, who was unhurt, to a nearby motel, after searching out a veterinarian for the dogs. He left my cousin at the motel, to return a few minutes later with his wife, who was carrying some hot food. The couple then drove my cousin to a service station, to which the trailer had been towed, so that she might retrieve any valuables left in the trailer and so that the animals could be looked after. The sheriff, incidentally, was off duty when he performed these services.

My cousin found that, although the trailer had also turned over, the birds were in their cages and unharmed. The tortoise was found under a pile of debris, also unharmed. The contents of the closets and drawers, however, and the furniture, food supplies, etc., had all been thrown into a heap on the floor.

The sheriff and his wife spent most of the night helping my cousin get settled and driving her to and from the trailer with her belongings and ours. And it was a good twenty-seven miles from the trailer to the motel. The following day, she was offered the use of a car, at no charge, by a local car dealer, to complete the job. At the motel, the owner allowed her the use of a room, also free of charge, in which to keep our belongings.

Meanwhile, at the hospital, I was under constant sedation in order to lessen the pain. During this period of half-wakefulness, I was dimly aware of being ministered to by doctors, nurses, and orderlies. On the fourth day, the amount of drugs was lessened, and my mind began to function again more or less normally. I had thought, while I was under sedation, that I had been dreaming when I saw that those who were caring for me were both Negro and white. Now I discovered that it had not been a dream at all, but that the staff was a fully integrated one. I would not have thought twice about this—except for the fact that I was in Georgia, supposedly one of the most vehemently segregationist states of the Union.

The patients, as well as the staff, were both Negro and white, and never once was any patient, regardless of color, shown anything less than the most complete respect and consideration. A week after the accident, I was able to get around in a wheelchair, and I observed accident cases, elderly patients, and newborn babies being cared for. Each was treated equally well, no matter what their color. There was no such thing as preference, or "special treatment," for the white patients to the detriment of the black ones. I was hardly prepared to find this matter-of-fact brotherhood in practice in the South, and in Georgia of all places. In fact, I had rarely seen it in the supposedly integrated Northern states.

I spent six weeks in Georgia, and in all that time I saw less segregation and less racial tension than I have seen on one city block in New York City. When I am confronted with such a surprising phenomenon, I usually do a "psychic meditation" on it—that is, using my psychic sense, I try to determine the causes and effects. I did so in this case, and the impression came to me that the racial conflict would, in a short period of time, be concentrated almost exclusively in the Northern cities, for there, and not in the much-maligned South, was the real obstacle to integration and equal rights for the black man. Newark and Detroit proved this out, I think, in 1967.

Because of the constant brainwashing that I had been subjected to in the North via radio, newspapers, television, books, plays, and films, I had come to believe that the South was, for the most part, made up of bigoted, prejudiced whites, and poor, oppressed, ignorant blacks. Quick to condemn what I believed was a true picture of life in the South, I had become—as do most people who have not seen for themselves—bigoted and prejudiced myself.

One of the friends I made in the hospital convinced me of this. Dr. Elaine Murphy was a patient-neighbor of mine, a middle-aged, white resident of South Carolina. Her work, in Columbia, is with deaf and dumb black children. The pay is negligible, and the work is arduous and heartbreaking. Dr. Murphy showed me slides of the children and of the school. It is a tumble-down shack, and Dr. Murphy and her white assistants live and work in frightful conditions trying to help the unfortunate children who are sent to the school.

With love, patience, and knowledge, Dr. Murphy and her staff have helped many black children to a better existence. "Before-and-after" slides of certain so-called hopeless cases showed beyond a doubt the great good that this lady and her friends are doing.

After being released from the hospital, we stayed at the local motel for several days in order to get our belongings together. I purchased another trailer for the trip back to New York. During this short period the many friends we had made did their best to be helpful, and we left finally with a great good feeling of well-being.

In short, the South I saw on this trip, and on a second, more extended (and less confining) one the following year, was not the legendary South seething with racial violence and hatred. It is true, of course, that there is some violence, some hatred, in the South, as there is wherever human beings live. But I know also, from firsthand experience, that there are many people in the South, both black and white, who live and work side by side with their neighbor, regardless of the color of his skin, and they do so in peace and contentment. Instead of the chaos and hostility that I had been taught to expect, I found only kindness, sympathy, and brotherhood among the many people that we met. An example may well be made of this for the benefit of the Northern cities, for a time of racial strife in the North is at hand.

From a spiritual point of view, I brought back from the South with me the conviction that I was, from that time, never to be alone again. There was another force—either within me or outside of myself—that would protect me and guide my life. I was to have constant proof of this.

We arrived back in New York City in January 1966. One evening shortly after that, I went to sleep after having draped across the foot of my bed a silk robe I had received as a Christmas gift. Many hours later I heard a deep, resonant voice calling me, as if in a dream: "Daniel, get up! Daniel, get up!"

I sat up with a start and looked quickly around the trailer, convinced that there was someone else there. A tall figure, dressed in a flowing garment, seemed to be standing on the other side of the room. At least, it appeared to be a figure of some kind, but I could not make out his (or its) features, as it was in a shadow.

"Who are you? What do you want?" I demanded. I was convinced that someone had broken into the trailer.

"Don't be afraid," the voice said. "I want you to get up out of your bed. Place your right foot on the floor, and you'll know the reason for my being here."

I was positive that this was a robbery of some sort, but, instinctively, I did as I was told and, kicking off the covers, I put my right foot on the floor. It touched something hot, smoldering. I reached down and picked up my silk robe. It had slipped off the bed during the night and landed on top of one of the heating vents located along the floor. The robe had been on the verge of bursting into flame.

The instant that I realized I had been protected, the figure disappeared. I have not seen it since, but I was certain at the time that I had not dreamed it—or had I?

A last word about the trailer and psychic phenomena. One weekend in February 1966 my mother came to visit me. I was still wearing my painful back brace day and night, and consequently I had trouble sleeping. At five o'clock in the morning, I was awakened from a light sleep by the sound of an unusually high wind raging outside. My mother, hearing me move about, got up also. The

wind was whistling around and beneath the trailer—
which, incidentally, was an Airstream (the Rolls-Royce of
trailerdom), with two separate rooms, a full bath, and a
complete kitchen. The outside was of aluminum siding,
and it was rounded at both ends to cut down on wind
resistance.

Mother and I sipped tea and talked awhile, until a
sudden and tremendous crashing sound interrupted our
conversation. Something had hit the back end of the
trailer. I went out into the darkness and found a piece of
metal lying across the back section of the trailer. A corru-
gated steel sun awning, thirty by eight feet, had been
ripped loose by the wind from a neighboring trailer fifty
feet away and had fallen directly on top of my trailer.

The next morning we discovered a huge dent in the
roof. The trailer next to ours had not been so fortunate. A
piece of awning had fallen on this trailer also and had
gone through the roof with such force that it had even
penetrated the floor.

The spot in which my trailer was standing was the same
spot in which I had kept my first trailer—that of Georgia-
accident fame. I had reserved the exact space in the
trailer court before we headed South, intending to park
there upon my return. The first trailer was not made of
metal, however, and its roof was of the same light material as the one on the trailer that the awning had pierced. If
I had returned in the original trailer, the awning would
have come right through into the bedroom. Again, I had
been protected. Three times in a short span, I had been
spared either death or serious injury. And each time,
psychic phenomena was involved.

Putting two and two together, it will not be difficult to
deduce that the more I gave of my gift, the more I
received in return, in both material and spiritual gain.

8

By the time of the experiences related in the preceding chapter, I had begun to make something of a "name" for myself among people interested in psychic phenomena, and I began to be approached to appear before not only Spiritualist audiences but also before the general public. In the beginning, most of these invitations were from radio "hosts" who were out to create an audience for themselves by having controversial guests, whom they intended to expose as frauds or otherwise to exploit. After several such frustrating experiences, I stopped accepting such invitations.

Television was the next step. An assistant on the *David Susskind Show* had attended a lecture I delivered under the auspices of the New York Parapsychology Forum, and as a result of the impression I made on him I was asked to submit to the interview described in the first chapter of this book. Thereafter, success, and a certain amount of fame, came quickly.

The reader who recalls my rather stormy childhood and the precarious nature of my relations with my family, touched on earlier in the book, will probably wonder how my success in such a bizarre field has affected my mother and father and my brothers. And this is probably as good a place as any to digress a bit and explain what the situation is today. First, however, one should remember that my family is an average, fairly normal one, with the attitudes, hierarchy of values, and "hang-ups" of most middle-class American families; which means that they have a low degree of tolerance for any deviation from the ordinary, and a high degree of incredulity when it comes to the occult or the mystic in any form.

With that background in mind, it is not hard to understand that my family generally believes that I have "gone off the deep end"—as would almost any family whose son became a professional psychic. In fact, knowing what their reaction would be, it was a full year after I had become a full-time psychic before I could get up the courage to tell them exactly what kind of work I was doing. Their lack of confidence in me during previous endeavors, and their conspicuous lack of encouragement, had made me overly cautious.

My mother actually is the only member of my family who has some sympathy for my work, and it took quite a bit of persuasion on my part to convince her that I was truly psychically gifted. At first she was hurt that I had become what to her must have seemed like a "fortune-teller." Being a very strict Catholic, she connected this work with that of the Devil or of other evil forces. Gradually, however, I was able to persuade her to attend several of my lectures and to watch the television programs I appeared on, and her skepticism lessened and her horror of the whole business abated.

What finally convinced her, I think, that I was not mad, or a fake, or in league with the Devil, was a series of predictions I made that she could neither challenge nor disregard. In the middle of 1965 (while I was still in my probationary period so far as my mother was concerned), she telephoned me and asked about a neighbor of hers.

"Can you tell me anything about Mrs. Oliskiw?"

As most people do when they want to test me, Mother gave me no clue as to the situation of Mrs. Oliskiw. It was a question out of the blue, and she wanted an answer out of the blue. I had not seen the lady in question for many years, but, fortunately, a psychic impression came.

"She's very ill, isn't she?" I asked. "I feel that she will have a stroke and go to the hospital. But she will get better and return home. Then, a short time after, she will have a second stroke and be rushed to the hospital again. This time, she will not recover, and she will die before the end of 1965."

Just before I left for Florida on that ill-fated trip, my mother called to say that Mrs. Oliskiw had had an attack and had been taken to the hospital, but that she was home again and apparently was all right. A few days later, however, while I was recuperating in the Hinesville hospital, I called my mother, and while we were talking she mentioned that Mrs. Oliskiw was very well, and that since the end of the year was less than two weeks away, it seemed, thank God, that my prediction had been wrong. But the following week, when I telephoned again, my mother reported that Mrs. Oliskiw had had a relapse, was rushed to the hospital, and had died just the day before. The day of her death was only a few days prior to the end of 1965.

One afternoon during 1965 I casually said to my mother, "Your nephew, George Toth, and his wife, will announce this September that they are going to have a baby."

George and his wife, when confronted with this bit of news, said that it was untrue. And, in fact, September rolled around, and there was no announcement.

"Aha," said my mother, "you were wrong!"

In May of 1966, however, George's wife presented him with a fine baby boy. The September that I had pegged for the announcement was nine months previous to the actual birth. For one reason or another George and his wife had kept the pregnancy secret until December 1965, when she was well into her fourth month.

I seem to have a special talent for knowing when children are going to be born into the family, long before the parents concerned even suspect it. In late 1966 I told my mother that my older brother's wife would have a third child during 1967. When Mother passed this information on, the couple laughed. "Not if I can help it," my sister-in-law said.

"We have two already," my brother announced, "and we don't want another one so soon."

Nonetheless, on August 13, 1967, I became an uncle for the third time.

Such happenings as these, trivial though they may seem to the outsider, carried great weight with my mother. Not only did my predictions about the family prove to be correct, but she could not believe that anything having to do with such things as grandchildren could possibly be all bad.

The job of convincing her that I had a true gift, and a

good one, was completed by several predictions that also concerned the family directly. At one of my psychic trance sessions, at which my mother was present, a voice addressed her: "Teresa, you must say a novena [a series of Catholic prayers that last for nine days] for your husband. Something terrible is coming up for him." The following week, my father stumbled while getting out of a car; he fell, and struck the curb, breaking his collarbone and cutting his face so badly that many stitches were required.

My mother was at one time very worried about the possibility of my younger brother going to Vietnam. At one of my lectures, during the period when I gave psychic impressions to the audience, I said to her: "Don't worry about William. He is going to be all right. Although he is in the reserves, he will be discharged within three months, and he will not have to go overseas."

Three months later, my brother received a medical discharge from the reserves because of a rheumatic condition.

Another time, my mother was ill and her doctor advised her to enter a hospital for surgery. "Don't go," I advised her. "This condition will clear up without any medical treatment. If you undergo the operation suggested, it will do you great harm."

One may imagine that the doctor concerned was not very pleased with this interference. But my mother trusted my psychic sense more than she did the doctor's diagnosis, and today she is perfectly well. The ailment disappeared as spontaneously as it had appeared.

My mother, as a result of her experiences with my psychic gifts, has become my most ardent supporter. She does not, however, attend my public showings too frequently. She claims that they make her nervous. Motherlike, she wants me to be correct one hundred percent of the time and is afraid of an occasional failure on my part.

So far as the rest of my family is concerned, our relations have improved appreciably since those difficult days of my childhood, and I get along well with them, individually and collectively. None of them, however, has been as understanding or as open-minded as my mother. My elder brother, for example, finds it difficult to accept the fact that I have a special talent of my own. He ridiculed my ambitions when I was interested in the theater, and he ridicules my work as a psychic. His feeling is that I shall bring disgrace to the family name.

My younger brother has shown surprising tolerance and even sympathy for something he does not understand. He wrote me a touching letter, explaining that, while he did not understand what I was doing, he appreciated that I had a right to do it so long as I truly believed in my gift. He urged me to forgive my elder brother's lack of understanding of what I was doing, suggesting that my elder brother did not have the sort of mind that could cope with the unknown or the intangible.

My father, on the other hand, does not seem to know quite what to make of the whole thing. So far as he is concerned, I am still in show business, though in a rather special kind of show business. When I appeared on Johnny Carson's *Tonight Show*, for example, his comment was: "Is that all he's going to do? Just sit there and tell people when they're going to move, or something? Isn't he even going to sing, or dance?"

My other relatives are either tolerant or else hide their intolerance under a blanket of silence. The general feeling among them is one of pity for my mother, who is destined to go through life afflicted with a son who is "not quite right" and who, worst of all, is going against the teachings of his Church.

As I developed my psychic gifts, there was also a noticeable dwindling in the number of my friends. I became in their eyes something of an "oddball," someone who knew everything about everyone—and who might Tell All. Hence, one had to be careful.

As usual, however, the best way to make friends is to be successful, and after my television "special" and my appearances on the *Tonight Show* and on the *David Susskind Show* there was a change in attitude.

I don't mean to sound cynical, for I am not that. The great joy in my life is contact with people and the gift that enables me to help them. Still, I cannot help feeling at present a certain resentment at the fact that family and friends, love, understanding, help, and encouragement have all come too late. It was before I was successful that

I needed them, not now. Acceptance is always welcome, of course, but when it comes late it is likely to be received with just a hint of resentment. Hopefully the passage of time will bring me the grace to overcome this vestige of selfishness.

9

In the preceding chapter I mentioned that it was while lecturing for the New York Parapsychology Forum that I came to the attention of Mr. David Susskind, and it was with my subsequent appearance on Mr. Susskind's television show that began my radio and TV career in the psychic field. If the truth be told, this apparently well-linked chain of cause and affect was actually pure accident, for it was by chance, and in spite of myself, that I spoke for the Forum at all that year.

The New York Parapsychology Forum is an institution founded almost half a century ago to foster interest in parapsychological phenomena. The Forum, in the person of its capable executive officer, Miss Ann Koernig, invites speakers from all over the world who specialize in some branch of parapsychological studies or in a related field. Thus it was that, in May of 1966, I received an invitation to address the Forum in the following November. I accepted. As it happened, when November rolled around I was in California. But, having accepted the invitation, I had no choice but to honor the commitment; and so, not without a good deal of grumbling, I traveled the three thousand miles from California to New York.

To say that I was "in California" seems innocent enough. But the fact is that I was still struggling mightily against my burgeoning career as a psychic, and I had gone to California determined to make one more attempt to find a career in show business by (ironically) crashing television. I still felt that show business would provide the most satisfying outlet for my gifts and the greatest personal happiness. Moreover, I was still miffed, I suppose, that my talents had as yet gone unrecognized in the theater.

Early in the summer of 1966, therefore, with my trailer again in tow, I headed for Los Angeles and, I hoped, television. My route was via the Atlantic seaboard to South Carolina and Georgia, where I visited friends made on my previous trip, then across the Southern and Southwestern states. The trip was an eye-opener. Never had I dreamed that this country contained such incredible natural beauty. The scenic splendors of the Southwest, of parts of Texas, New Mexico, and Arizona, are beyond human imagining. An excursion, on muleback, no less, to the bottom of the Grand Canyon, was an esthetic and spiritual experience that I shall never forget.

Because of my somewhat extreme personal and psychic beliefs, I have been accused of being everything from an anarchist to a Communist. I am neither. I love this country and what it was meant to stand for with a great passion. On that trip, my love for America was confirmed. God has been unbelievably kind to this country, granting not only liberty and justice, but a land of incomparable natural beauty. I have lived most of my life near New York City, and I never imagined that the United States contained such wonders. For all my love and admiration for this country, however—or rather, because of it—I cannot help holding and expressing opinions that, to some, seem at least unorthodox and perhaps even unpatriotic. The reason is that I feel psychically—and quite strongly—that the United States is now in the gravest danger of its history; and it is not, as in the past, a danger from without, but a danger from within. The vibrations are at a perilously low level, and unless they are drastically improved in the near future there is no power on earth that will be able to save this beloved land from the destruction that has been predicted for it.

This feeling of impending doom was heightened in Los Angeles. I have read and heard many predictions of destruction with regard to that city. I have even made some myself. But I was unprepared for the actuality of the city, for its total devotion to gross materialism. Los Angeles' vibrations are the lowest of any city that I have visited. To a psychic, a visit to Los Angeles is like a tour of a morgue, a place inhabited by bodies drained of their souls and without even a spark of spiritual life. The smog, which hovers, like a symbol of the wrath that is to come, over each of the cities that are marked out for destruction, was intense throughout the five months I spent in that city.

Los Angeles' world of television and movies is as depressing and spiritually empty as the city itself. It is a world overpopulated by zombie-like aging "juveniles" and "ingenues," still hoping, always hoping, for the big "break" that will never come; by beautiful girls and handsome boys from little Midwestern towns, posing in the streets and bars and drugstores, waiting to be "discovered" and not noticing that the streets of Los Angeles are littered with the bleaching bones of girls and boys more beautiful and more handsome—and more talented—than they. It is a sad place, and a bleak one. And, above all, a heartbreaking one.

For months I knocked at the doors of agents, producers, directors. I haunted the studios. But all to no avail. My New York credits were laughed at. (In New York, agents, directors, and producers laugh at California credits. The rivalry between the two so-called art centers is as childish as it is unbelievable.) There were a few opportunities, of course; chances to sell either one's soul or one's body, or perhaps both, for a moment's appearance in a film or a commercial. It was too high a price to pay, even for the satisfaction of one's ego.

In the midst of this corruption, I had one psychic experience in all the months I spent in California, and it was an experience of a very personal nature. My car was being repaired, and I was waiting one day for a bus to take me back to the trailer court. As I was standing there, a strange feeling came over me. I felt so dizzy that it was necessary for me to sit down for a moment. About twenty feet from the bench where I was sitting there was a small driveway, out of which I saw emerging a hearse and a few cars. Suddenly, as if impelled by an exterior force, I got up and entered the driveway. At the end of it was the smallest cemetery I have ever seen, composed of a few crypts. A man was taking pictures of a crypt at the edge

of the tiny cemetery. I watched him as he walked around
the crypt, taking shots from every possible angle. Finally,
he had had enough and closed the camera. Then he
noticed me watching him and walked over to me.

"You'd never believe she was in there, would you?" he
asked.

"Who?" I mumbled, thinking that the man was probably unbalanced.

"Who?" he said. "Marilyn—"

I didn't give him a chance to finish saying the name. I
dashed over to the crypt and read: "Marilyn Monroe
1926-1962."

I realized that I had been led to that cemetery, to that
tomb. I have never had such a feeling of loneliness as that
which seemed to emanate from it. It was indeed impossible to believe that such a vibrant, lovely creature was
enclosed in the block of cement that was her crypt.

How mysterious it seemed. I had been led to the spot
that was Marilyn Monroe's last resting place. I had had no
intention ever of visiting her grave. Indeed, I never visit
cemeteries, even cemeteries where are interred those who
have been dear to me. And, in this instance, the dizziness
and the feeling of being ill left me as soon as I entered
the cemetery. It was obvious to me that the strange
"bond" between Miss Monroe and me existed still. I
returned home in a daze.

November was drawing near and there was still no sign
of any worthwhile theatrical work. Remembering the date
of the Parapsychology Forum lecture to have been set for
the fifteenth, I reluctantly decided to return to New York
and fulfill my commitment and, at the same time, to visit
my family for the Thanksgiving holiday.

The larger part of my lecture at the Parapsychology
Forum was taken up with the rendering of readings for
the audience. The very first impression I received that
evening concerned Miss Koernig, president of the Forum.
(She was quite surprised, and explained later that seldom,
if ever, did the guest speakers single her out.)

"Miss Koernig," I said from the rostrum, "I believe this
message is for you. I do not usually get numbers or
addresses, but in this case I receive four digits very strongly. I feel they are part of an address. Can you place this:

one, one, one—and the last digit seems to be a seven. Do you recognize it?"

"Yes," she answered. "I recognize it."

"I do not get the name of the street," I continued. "But I perceive two capital M's. Could it be Minnesota—Minneapolis, Minnesota?"

"Yes, I know that address," Miss Koernig answered matter-of-factly. (Miss Koernig always says everything matter-of-factly.)

"You will soon hear of a health problem there concerning someone close to you. But the situation will be under control. You must not worry about this when you hear of it, no matter how bad it may seem at the time."

Months later, when I again appeared before the Forum at the Wellington Hotel in Manhattan, Miss Koernig announced that during my lecture I had received the address of close relatives in Minnesota and that, a few days after that lecture, she had received word of a serious illness among them. The situation, however, was, as I had said, under control.

I had never met Miss Koernig socially, and I knew nothing of her personal life or her family. In fact, I did not even know that she had relatives, much less that they lived in Minneapolis.

The day following my November appearance with Miss Koernig's organization, the David Susskind office telephoned me. Shortly thereafter—after the grueling examination described in the first chapter—I made my first television appearance, on Mr. Susskind's show.

The reader is already aware of the predictions that I made during the course of that show, and it should be noted that a large percentage of those forecasts have to do with international or national, as opposed to personal, affairs. I should explain that I have been encouraged by radio and television producers to predict events in these areas, since, they feel, audience interest is particularly high there. World affairs, however, is not my forte. I work best with individuals, on a personal level. It is much easier for me to sense vibrations while speaking directly with a person. Moreover, there are so many changing vibrations in world affairs that it is very difficult to make long-range predictions. If I were confronted, face-to-face, with the men involved in any given international situation, the results would be more accurate. Though my percentage of accuracy in world affairs is high, it is much higher in the personal readings that I have given.

Apparently, however, the television executives were right about "audience interest" in the international situation, for my appearance evoked a nation-wide response so strong that Mr. Susskind concluded that he should make a television "special" about my gift.

By the time the audience's reaction was received by Mr. Susskind, I was back in California. In the face of this new opportunity, however, I decided to return to New York permanently. The taping of the special, and the amount of work that would be required both before and after such a program (plus, I confess, the fact that I had not even cracked, let alone crashed, television in California), seemed to necessitate my presence in that city. I had decided, in effect, to take the opportunity afforded by the special. It was the only way open to me—therefore, I concluded, it must be intended that I take advantage of it. So, I moved back to New York.

The task of making the show, and the enormous amount of responsibility entailed, almost drove me into a state of complete exhaustion. Finally, however, "Daniel Logan: a Man Who Predicts Your Future" was shown on television on April 18, 1967, and was repeated the following Sunday, April 23.

Mr. Susskind had invited two guests to appear on the program with me: Dr. Ira Progoff, and Dr. Henry Puharich, two noted specialists in the field of extrasensory perception. As competent and well intentioned as those gentlemen were, I could not help feeling that their contribution was a waste of time, since all they said in effect was that there was such a thing as psychic phenomena and that psychic phenomena were being studied at universities and colleges. At the time, I was distressed that so much time was taken up by them in the middle of the program; and my fears were confirmed when the Nielsen ratings were received. The ratings showed that the program started off with a very high percentage of listeners, but the percentage diminished during the middle part of show, when the good doctors were on. My feeling was, and is, that people are interested in practical demonstration and not in erudite discussion. And that feeling is not based on psychic sense but on show-biz sense.

I am also opposed to the almost inevitable "testing" that one encounters on television and radio. I have already described the enormous waste of energy that this involves for the psychic—energy that could be much better, and more convincingly, employed in demonstrating one's gift. Moreover, attempting to test, or measure, psychic phenomena by material methods is exactly like cutting open a body and expecting to find a soul; psychic phenomena is, by its nature, spiritual, and it is not susceptible to material methodologies. For this reason, such tests usually do not work—and then the testers say, "Aha. Just as we thought. There's nothing there." Whereas, all they have proved in fact is that their material methods do not apply to spiritual qualities. Only when testing utilizes spiritual methods to measure spiritual qualities will headway be made.

Despite all of these objections to the way that radio and television shows are run, I still appear on both media. The reason is simple: I want to leave a permanent, indisputable record of my psychic accomplishments. These appearances are, to my mind, demonstrations of my gift, and they are therefore the only tests that really count. And they are the only tests to which I shall ever submit.

The evening we taped the special for Mr. Susskind, the studio audience had been selected at random from the files of the Susskind office and was composed of people who had written to the station expressing an interest in psychic phenomena. It was, therefore, a most receptive and cooperative audience, which made it possible for us to accomplish a good deal; in fact, we taped much more than it would have been possible to show in a one-hour program.

In addition to the appearance of the two doctors and the consultation with Betsy von Furstenberg already described, the program—the rest of it, in fact—consisted of readings given to members of the audience. The procedure was simple; I merely walked down into the audience and selected people at random. Unfortunately, most of the material that had to be edited out in order to keep the program within its one-hour limit came from these readings. And I thought that much of the material that was thus eliminated was better and more interesting than what was left in.

In one segment that was cut out, I asked the audience if there were not two people present with the name of Smith. Two persons sitting at opposite ends of the studio— a man and a woman—raised their hands.

"I would like to speak with the lady named Smith," I said, and the lady stood up. "Madame," I went on, "I feel that you do not live in Manhattan. You come from a short distance away. Is that correct?"

"Yes."

"I feel that you come from Queens, New York—near Flushing; from my part of the country. Do you come from Whitestone?"

"I live there now, yes," she answered.

"Do I know you? Have we met before?"

"No."

"You live in a red brick house, and the reason you are in Manhattan has something to do with a child, a daughter. But it is a very personal matter, and you don't wish me to speak of it in public. Is this correct?"

"Absolutely," the lady exclaimed.

I then singled out a very attractive young lady. "You are very worried about someone, a man. And you are worried about something that has to do with employment for him. He is an actor, isn't he?"

"Yes," the lady said, "and he's right here with me." A young man stood up next to her.

"You are thinking about an agent," I went on, "something about an agent—whether or not you should sign with him. There are two agents, aren't there, and you must choose between them?"

"Yes," she said. "Which one should he choose?"

"He should choose the one with the glasses, the darker of the two."

"Thank you. We know which one you mean."

The editors should, I feel, have left those readings in, for they were most effective. Those that were left in for the television showing dealt mostly with such personal problems as employment, business, and health. The following reading is fairly typical of what was shown.

"I would like to speak with the lady in the second row."

The lady stood up.

"Your husband is having problems in his business."

"Yes, that's so."

"These problems also involve family relationships," I said. "There are two people around him, relatives, that are not to be trusted. Your husband feels that the problem has now been taken care of satisfactorily. The truth is, however, that if he is not very careful in the next few months the same thing will happen again."

"That is exactly what I've thought all along," the woman said.

"One of the difficulties here is that there is a great deal of jealousy involved."

"I know that too," the lady said. "I've been trying to tell him this." She was elated that a complete stranger had confirmed her own impressions.

Another impromptu consultation occurred when a young man got up and challenged me. "You're being pretty general in your statements, and I'd like to have you do something more specific. For example, can you tell me the name of the rock 'n' roll band that I'm thinking of?"

"That is mind reading," I answered. "I don't do that." Mind reading, in my book, falls under the heading of "testing." It is an interesting parlor game, but it is useless and meaningless in the sense that it does no good for anyone concerned; that is, no one benefits from it. And there is not much point to being psychic if one is going to use one's gift for amusement rather than for helping and guiding others.

"But everything you've said is so general—" the young man went on.

"All right. I'll be more specific for you. You're studying writing of some kind, aren't you? You will become a writer."

The youth's mouth fell open. "I'm studying journalism," he responded.

"Within the next ten years you will be working for the New York *Times*. I hope that's specific enough for you."

A week previous to the taping of the show, an assistant producer said that he thought it would be a good idea to have, as the opening segment of the show, a group of people come on—people to whom I had given private readings—and tell about the fulfillment of prophecies I had made to them.

I spent the next week trying to talk clients and friends into going on the air. Most of them quite understandably did not want to go on television and talk about their personal affairs. Others said that they would be happy to appear, but that they were deathly afraid of television cameras. I had to make approximately one hundred telephone calls in order to get together a few people whom the assistant producer felt were necessary. When I finally had the required number, I turned the list over to the assistant producer, who screened the persons involved. One of my clients even came in from California to help me out. At the very last minute, however, I was told that the assistant producer had changed her mind. She did not think that my guests had such "dramatic" stories to tell, after all. Something stranger than my psychic gift is the fact that anything at all is ever accomplished in television.

The response to my television special was overwhelming, at least to me. I received over ten thousand letters, telegrams, and other communications in a very short time. Almost every one of them was from someone requesting a private consultation. And most of the people who wrote mentioned that they had never believed in clairvoyance before, but that the proof of my gift was in its demonstration and therefore could not be disbelieved.

My next television appearance was on Johnny Carson's *Tonight Show*. I received almost no prior notice for the show; in fact, I was called and invited on the very afternoon that the show was to be taped, and I was told that I must go on that night or not at all. I consented, even though it was against my better judgment to do so. My psychic impression was that my appearance on the show would not be as effective as it should. Being human, however, I felt that if I was really going to do this work and gain some recognition for it, then this opportunity for exposure was too good to pass up.

I arrived at the studio an hour before taping, as requested. The first forty-five minutes of the hour was occupied in watching people running up to me backstage to

ask me who I was and what I was doing there. About
fifteen minutes before taping time, the secretary of the
show turned up and established my status as a guest.

By this time my nerves were considerably frayed, and
the situation was not helped by what was to come. The
Tonight Show runs for ninety minutes. I was made to wait
until the last ten minutes before coming out. A segment
preceding mine consisted of one of Mr. Carson's special
pieces of material, in which he dons a turban and, as
questions are put to him, essays supposedly funny psychic
answers. My impression is that the routine is generally
funny, but that night it seemed particularly uncalled for in
that Mr. Carson had invited a guest who took this sort of
work seriously. To make matters worse, Mr. Carson's
routine had been preceded by a show remarkable for its
low humor and by the peculiar gifts of a scantily clad
young woman who seemed to specialize in muttering tor-
rid songs.

My impulse was to leave, simply to walk out. But I
restrained myself, not wanting it to appear as though I
was "copping out." At last I was announced, and went on
amid a torrent of skepticism and unjustified clowning. My
psychic impression was that Mr. Carson does not like, and
does not want to have on his show, psychics of any kind,
but that public demand and its subsequent pressures on
the network require him to invite one from time to time.

The only person I could reach that evening was another
guest, Miss Joan Rivers, who had worked for me at my
Greenwich Village nightclub a few years previously. I
had lost touch with Miss Rivers in the interim, but she
remained a basically empathetic person and was the
only one who did not block me. She was quite surprised
to see me appear in the capacity of a psychic, since
she had had no indication during our previous contact
that I was interested in anything but show business.

"There has been a death in your family very recently," I
told Miss Rivers. "You are still very upset about it."

"That's amazing," she said. "I just heard about a death
in the family this morning."

"It was on the in-law side of the family," I continued.

"That's quite true."

Then it was Mr. Carson's turn. I told him that his eldest

son would eventually go into writing. He denied this, cutting me off quite abruptly and telling me that his son was going to be a professional golfer. He did not give me time to explain it was about golf that the boy would eventually write. But by this time I was past caring about the future of Mr. Carson's son.

After the show, Mr. Ed McMahon, Mr. Carson's sidekick on the program, came over to me and asked if I could tell him anything.

"Yes," I said. "There seems to be something about another interest you have, an interest other than this show. You are worried about it. Actually, at this time it could go either way—either fail or succeed. But I can tell you that, if it is to succeed, there must be a change in personnel. There is someone involved who is wrong, who should not be involved. You must get rid of someone."

"That makes sense," he said gratefully. "Thank you."

And that was the whole of my experience with Mr. Carson and the *Tonight Show*. There was time for little else.

The most gratifying experience that I have had on the air was on CBS radio, when I made four appearances on *The Talk of New York* during the spring and summer of 1967. The hostess of this show was the gracious Carol Reed.

My first appearance was on May 16. Miss Reed seemed a trifle skeptical of my talent, but she was always polite and considerate and most generous in listening to her guests. On the air, she asked me if I could tell her something about her own affairs.

"Did you once live near the East River, a few years back? Near the United Nations?"

"My goodness, yes," she answered. "In Tudor City, a block away from the United Nations. But that was almost ten years ago."

"I get the impression of 'United Nations' very strongly from you. In a short time, you will be asked to do some work for that organization."

"That's interesting," she said. "But I can't pretend I really believe it. I've never worked for them, and I can't imagine what they'd want me for."

(Exactly one month later, Miss Reed was called by the United Nations and asked to do a job for them.)

"I feel that you do not presently live in the city. You live in a house in the country. But you have been thinking about getting an apartment in the city in addition to your home in the country."

"That's marvelous! No one could possibly have known that. I was just thinking about that today, and I haven't even talked to my husband about it yet. Traveling back and forth from the city is so tiring, especially when I work late hours, that I was thinking of getting an apartment where I could stay sometimes, when it got too bad."

Miss Reed was easy to "read," because she is very much at ease and comfortable in manner. She then brought in members of her staff for readings also. In addition, I was asked to answer telephone calls from the public, as phoning in to Miss Reed during her show is part of the format. It was the first time I had given readings via telephone.

After the program I met the producer of the show, Mr. Harvey Vincent. He apparently was impressed with my demonstration while on the air, for he asked for a private reading.

"You have been offered another job, not with CBS," I said. "It would be wise for you to turn down this offer. It wouldn't work out, and you would regret having accepted."

(Some weeks later, Mr. Vincent told me that the job that he had been offered, and that he was seriously considering until I had discouraged him, had fizzled out.)

"Tell me, are you planning at present to work in any other related medium?" I asked during the reading.

"No, I'm not."

"Nonetheless, you will be working in a related medium within the next six months."

(Almost exactly six months from the date of the reading, Mr. Vincent began working as the producer of a television show.)

During the course of the reading, Mr. Vincent also asked me to tell him what future he had with CBS. He had been associated with that network for eight years, and he had every hope of continuing on to bigger and better things with them.

"Do you wish me to be completely honest?" I asked.

"Yes, of course. Completely."

"There is no future for you with this station. I see nothing for you at CBS after a very short time."

(Mr. Vincent was visibly upset by this. But several months later, CBS became New York's second major all-news station, and many people whose services were no longer required were let go, as their shows were being canceled. Mr. Vincent was one of these unfortunate people.)

Mr. Vincent's wife is an opera singer. He wanted to know whether or not he should take his wife to Europe and try to establish her in opera there. He felt that it would be advantageous to Mrs. Vincent's career to do so.

"You must not go now," I answered. "If you do, you will lose out on a great deal here. There will be many opportunities for Mrs. Vincent and for you in this country, and you will miss them if you go to Europe. I also see your wife having a child."

The opportunities I spoke of did present themselves to Mr. and Mrs. Vincent, and they are very happy to have followed my advice. In early 1968 Mrs. Vincent became pregnant.

My dealings with Mr. Vincent illustrate, I think, my reasons for feeling that my most important and accurate work is done with individuals, rather than at the level of world affairs.

In August 1967 Carol Reed was taping the pilot film of a planned television series, and she asked me to be the first guest on her new program. I consented. The show, which was being produced by Ron Cochran, the news commentator, was to consist of four people from the audience who were to join Miss Reed and me on the stage, and to each of whom I was to give a brief reading.

One lady who came forward gave her name as Margaret Lund. I felt that she was not using her real name.

"Somehow," I said, "I am receiving the name Alice—or something similar to Alice. Isn't that your real name?"

"No," the lady replied, "my real name is Margaret."

"Is that really the name you use?" I persisted. "Aren't you usually called something else?"

"Well, sometimes I'm called by my nickname, Peggy. But not Alice."

"You don't use the name Alice, or something similar to it?" I asked for the third time. I was persistent because I was absolutely sure that the lady was not giving her real name.

"I have a cousin named Alice, but that's all I can tell you about the name."

When we had finished the tape, Mr. Cochran ran forward and excitedly told us, "My God, you were absolutely right, Daniel. After the lady went back to her seat, it dawned on her that you must have been picking up something about her last name. Her real last name was too similar to that of another person on the show, and she was asked to give her maiden name when she came up to the stage. Her maiden name is Margaret Lund, just as she said. But her married name—which is the name she ordinarily uses—is Malice. Margaret Malice! And you said you were picking up Alice or something like it."

It always amuses me slightly when people (who have hired me because I am psychic) are flabbergasted if I come up with something psychic.

In the fall of 1967 I made two appearances on the *Barry Gray Show* over New York's WMCA radio station. Mr. Gray has been on the air for over seventeen years, and he is as renowned for his vitriol as he is for his stark candor with respect to his guests.

My experience on the *Tonight Show* had taught me a lesson, and I realized that I would be much better off with Mr. Gray if I went on his show with a trick up my sleeve. If they wanted to play games, I decided, I could do the same.

I was scheduled to appear with Barry Gray on October 3, 1967, which was a Tuesday. On the preceding Saturday, I devised a plan. I had originally been contacted by Mr. Gray's producer, Miss Lilia Rollantz, who had asked me to appear on the second half of the program, from midnight until one o'clock. There would be another guest on the segment which ran from eleven to midnight, as is the usual procedure. Now, hoping to turn up some scheme which would prove my talent to Mr. Gray, I meditated and got the strong impression that, at the very last moment, Miss Rollantz would call and ask me to appear on Mr. Gray's program during the first segment—from eleven o'clock to midnight—because the other guest would be unable to make it.

The problem, then, was what to do with this bit of psychic information. On Monday morning I went to the office of the New York *Times* and had them run an ad in the Tuesday edition of the paper, with my photograph, stating that I would appear on Mr. Gray's program from eleven to midnight. I would therefore have proof that I had received this information psychically, for the deadline for ads in the Tuesday paper was Monday noon. It was a somewhat expensive scheme, but it would be worth it to prove to Mr. Gray, and to the skeptics listening at home, that there was indeed such a thing as psychic phenomena.

On Tuesday, in the late afternoon, the telephone rang. It was Miss Rollantz. "Daniel," she began.

I interrupted. "You've called to tell me your other guest couldn't make it, and you want to know if I can go on at eleven o'clock instead of midnight. Yes, I can."

"You're kidding," she said. "You must be kidding. How could you have known? You didn't even know who the other guest was."

"I knew about it last Saturday."

"But I just found out about it a few minutes ago!" She was shocked.

On the air, Mr. Gray was quite impressed with the ad. Although he was not completely convinced of my gift, he was not as skeptical as he usually is with people who claim psychic ability. In fact, he was quite gentlemanly.

"You have two children," I told him, "a boy and a girl. The girl is very artistic and is working in a creative line. She is having difficulty at this time with an employment situation, with her job within the organization—there is a change, a new position within the organization."

"That's interesting," Mr. Gray admitted, "because she works for a monthly magazine and has just taken on a new job there; naturally there is some anxiety involved."

On the second program Mr. Gray and I discussed politics. At the time, former child star Shirley Temple Black was running for Congress from the 11th Congres-

sional District in California. "What do you see in the
future for Shirley Temple?" Mr. Gray asked.

"She won't win," I answered flatly.

Mr. Gray, almost laughing, said, "My friend, that would
indeed be a surprise. That county, San Mateo, is probably
the most politically set county in the whole country. It's a
sure thing that she'll win. In fact, she can't lose."

On November 14, 1967, Shirley Temple Black lost the
primary election to her fellow Republican, Paul
McCloskey.

In the early part of 1968, on the NBC radio show *The
Long John Nebel Show* and on a local Manhattan TV
show, I predicted the correct winners of the 1967 Academy
Awards. This included the best picture, the four acting
and supporting acting awards, and the director award.
(As a matter of interest, I would like to make a future
prediction here that the singer-actress Barbra Streisand
will win an Academy Award.)

The radio and television shows that I have been on
have all been difficult, and some of them have been
outright unpleasant and unsatisfactory. But they are all,
the bad ones as well as the good ones, demonstrations of
psychic phenomena. And, for that reason if for no other,
they are important to me and, I would like to think, to the
future of extrasensory perception in this country.

10

It should be clear from what I have said throughout this
book that I believe firmly that everyone is psychic to some
extent, that everyone possesses a "sixth sense." That belief
is based, at least in part, on the fact that most people
seem to have had, at one time or another, at least one
experience that seems explainable only as an instance of
extrasensory perception. (Often, they do not tell even their

close friends about such experiences for fear of being ridiculed. But since I am "in the business," I suppose I am a natural confidant in this respect.) Most of my own friends, for example—some of whom are fascinated by every aspect of parapsychology, but others of whom are not particularly interested—have told me of psychic phenomena in which they themselves were involved.

One such friend is Treva Silverman, a successful television writer in California. Treva does not profess to be psychic, nor has she ever said anything to make me believe that she possesses an unusual degree of psychic ability—except in one instance. On that occasion Treva and I were talking long-distance (she in California, I in New York) during the early part of 1967. Suddenly, in midsentence, Treva stopped talking. After a moment of silence, I asked, "Treva, are you there?"

"Yes," she replied, "I'm here. It's just that—well, the thought suddenly came to me again. It's something that keeps popping into my mind, for no reason."

"What thought?"

"The three astronauts, Grissom, White, and Chaffee. I have the strangest feeling that something is going to happen to them, and I can't get rid of the feeling. I think they're going to be killed."

"That's a strange thought to have," I remember saying. I myself had no psychic response to the thought. Nonetheless, exactly four days from the time that Treva and I had spoken, the accident occurred which took the lives of the three astronauts in their capsule.

Another friend who has had psychic experiences is Victoria Fodor, widow of the noted psychiatrist and parapsychologist Nandor Fodor, who, unlike Treva Silverman, is most interested and involved in the subject of extrasensory perception. At the time of Dr. Fodor's sudden and wholly unexpected death by heart failure, there occurred a series of incidents which, as a whole, can be explained only through the intervention of psychic forces.

On a Sunday, exactly seven days before he died, Nandor Fodor, his wife, their daughter and son-in-law all were playing cards at the Fodor home. During the course of the evening, one card from the deck was inexplicably lost, and a thorough search failed to turn it up.

Seven days later, at 11:50 (the digits 1, 1, and 5 equal 7), Mrs. Fodor returned home from the hospital where her husband had just died. On a sudden and quite strong impulse, she went to one of the small armchairs that the family had used while playing cards and lifted the cushion. Beneath the cushion she found the missing card—the seven of spades. Then she recalled that her husband had been using that chair the evening of the card game.

It is notable that the card was a seven, that Dr. Fodor died seven days after somehow dropping the card under the cushion, that the hospital room number in which he died was 907 (9 plus 7 equals 16; 1 plus 6 equals 7), and that Fodor died in his seventieth year, on May 17, on the seventh day of the week.

Other events occurred during the week preceding Fodor's death that caused his family to feel that he was at least subconsciously aware of his approaching demise, and that he subconsciously posted an announcement of his death by dropping the seven of spades where his wife would not find it until after the event. On the previous Tuesday, for example, Fodor had told a patient, who had a neurotic fear of heart trouble, that he should not worry. "Just last night," Fodor told him, "I myself dreamed that I had had a heart attack and died. But, as you can see, I'm still alive and well."

Only three days before Fodor's death, his daughter, who is an artist, felt extremely restless and was looking about for an object to use as a model for a painting. Her eye fell upon a statue of her father that Mrs. Fodor had sculpted some time before. It seemed to her that the work would look better if refinished in a lighter tone. So, she immediately began removing the old finish and, in the process, she remembers being struck by the strong thoughts of death aroused in her by the original gray finish of the statue.

Similarly, during the entire week preceding May 17, Fodor's son-in-law had the uneasy feeling that he would soon become somehow involved in funeral arrangements. And many of Fodor's friends and patients had dreams of a precognitive nature during the week preceding his death.

Several weeks after Dr. Fodor's death, Mrs. Fodor telephoned to ask me to come to dinner. Her husband had been at work on a book when he died, and Mrs. Fodor explained that she wanted to talk to me about the possibility of my completing the book. It was, she said, an impression that she received quite strongly, and she was certain that it was her husband's wish that I be the one to finish his work. A few days later I went to the Fodor apartment for dinner. As we sat discussing the book and the circumstances of Dr. Fodor's death, it dawned upon me that a strange coincidence was once more involved.

"How did you arrive at this particular day in deciding when to ask me to dinner?" I asked.

"I? I didn't decide. You know perfectly well that I've asked you several times, but you were always too busy to come. Finally, I just took the first day that you were free. Why?"

"Do you know what today's date is?"

"Not offhand, no."

"It is July 7, 1967. The seventh day of the seventh month, in the seventh year—and in inviting me to dinner you said 'seven o'clock.' It seems that the number seven is again connected with the death of your husband!"

If the number seven had simply cropped up two or three times in connection with Fodor's death, it could have been explained by the laws of chance. But to have that digit continuing to recur time after time, before, during, and after the time of his death, seems to me to suggest that it was more than chance or coincidence. Dr. Fodor himself was a brilliant man, with great strength of character and mind, and a man dedicated to the exploration of the mysteries of parapsychology. It is my opinion that his vibrations in the atmosphere continued to influence those to whom he was close during his life—as evidenced by Mrs. Fodor's apparently spontaneous compulsion to raise the cushion of the chair where her husband had been sitting a week before, by her conviction that her husband intended that I be the one to complete work on his book, and so forth. The number seven itself probably has no intrinsic significance here—except for the fact that it has always been regarded, in all parts of the world and by all religions, as a sacred and "mystic" number, and a perfect and indivisible quantity (e.g., the Seven Tablets of Creation of Babylon, the seven-branched can-

delabra of Judaism, the seven sacraments of Roman Ca-
tholicism, the monotonous recurrence of that numeral in the
Book of the Revelation, etc.). It is consequently regarded
as "the perfect psychic number"—a circumstance of which
Dr. Fodor was certainly aware. It is therefore my interpretation that the number seven was used by Fodor's soul, or
vibrations, as both a means of identifying himself (beginning with the selection of the seven of spades to announce
his death) and of linking together the events that were to
follow his death by the recurrence of the numeral.

Perhaps I may be pardoned for dwelling at such length
on the psychic circumstances surrounding Dr. Fodor's
death. The fact is that death is one of the great preoc-
cupations of mankind, and it is probably for this reason
that death figures so often in psychic phenomena and that
psychic phenomena so often occur shortly before or after
the moment of death. It seemed to me that the wealth of
connected psychic manifestations surrounding Dr. Fodor's
demise merited more than passing mention as an illustration of that fact.

I myself have often had premonitions of the forthcoming death of a person, and frequently the person in question was not someone whom I knew personally. In 1966,
for example, when plans were being made for Spencer
Tracy to make the film *Guess Who's Coming to Dinner*
with Katharine Hepburn and Sidney Poitier, I read an
announcement regarding the project. I immediately had a
very strong impression that the film would be an award-
winning one. But, in the next instant, I knew with abso-
lute certainly that Mr. Tracy, although he would complete
the film, would not live to see it released, and I communi-
cated this impression to a group of my students.

Similarly, in the first days of December 1967, I came
across a photograph of Francis Cardinal Spellman of New
York. There was a very strong feeling of death emanating
from the picture. I told my mother, who was with me at
the time, that the cardinal would die within the next few
weeks. A few days later, Spellman was dead of a massive
cerebral hemorrhage.

Premonitions of death are not experienced exclusively
by professional psychics. On the contrary, it is one of the
most common manifestations of the latent psychic sense

with which all mankind is endowed. My friend William McCarthy, for example, once announced that he felt very strongly that his father would not live out the current year. He consulted with a medium, who confirmed his impression and even ventured to name the day on which he would die. William described the medium's impression to me afterward, but he added, "I don't believe that he will die on the date that the medium specified. My own feeling is that he will die at a different time." And he told me on what day he felt his father would die. William's father did die during the course of the year, and the day of his death fell within a week of the date that William had predicted. William's father had been ill for many years, and it was not impossible that he might continue for many years yet. There was no reason for William to feel that this particular year would be the one of his father's passing—no reason, except for the "sixth sense" that allowed him to know not only the year, but almost the exact date, months before the actual occurrence.

One of the vivid memories of my childhood concerns a woman of our neighborhood who had an uncanny faculty for foreseeing a death. It was a gift, however, that was beclouded with superstitious beliefs. "I saw a crow in the back yard this morning. He was screaming so much that I chased him away. I wonder who's going to die now?" she would say.

I recall at least six or seven occasions when this woman told my mother that she "saw a crow"—and, in each instance, a death followed shortly thereafter in the neighborhood. I have often wondered since whether there was in fact a crow (crows are quite rare in that section of New York), or whether the crow was not a hallucination produced by the woman's psychic sense in order to be understood by the woman's untutored mind.

On several occasions I have received unexpected, and valuable, advice of a psychic nature from people who make no claim to being psychic. At one of my lectures in New York, I was asked by a lady to give her a private reading. I set a date for the lady, whose name is Celia Hartman, and during the course of the reading Miss Hartman asked for my telephone number, explaining that she would like to call me from time to time. She did indeed call several times, and during these calls she would often spontaneously predict an event that was to occur. On one such occasion, she told me that she felt that I must not leave the city during August of that year. "I have a feeling about a television show," she explained. "If you go away, you'll miss out on it; and it would be very good for you to appear on that particular show. You must stay in the city during August."

It was in August of that year (1967) that I was approached by Miss Carol Reed and asked to appear in the pilot of her television show. Had I not listened to Miss Hartman and had I accepted either one of the two out-of-town engagements offered for the month of August, I should surely not have been able to appear on Miss Reed's show.

At another time, Miss Hartman spoke to my mother on the telephone and told her that she had a "strange feeling" about my father—that he would be ill, but that my mother was not to worry for it would not be serious. It was about a week later that my father had the accident which involved his falling from a moving car (described earlier in the book). And it was at the same time as she received Miss Hartman's warning that my mother heard the same warning from me while I was in trance.

Another friend who has been psychically helpful is Dana Hutchenson, a barber who was one of the pioneers in the field of men's hair-styling. In addition to his professional concerns, Dana is interested in hypnotism, astrology, and especially in the ancient form of divination called I-Ching (which is based upon a Pythagorean belief that "the world is built upon the power of numbers" and in which the future is foretold by a complex system of numerical interpretation). Dana was cutting my hair one day when I mentioned that I had an appointment in the near future with an executive of ABC television, and that ABC apparently was interested in me as a possible subject for a television show. By the next time I saw Dana, he had worked out the situation with I-Ching and was able to tell me what to expect from the ABC executive.

"From the results received of the I-Ching," he said, "I would say you're in for a rough time. The meeting will be tiring, and it won't go as you want it to. So, don't expect too much. There will be problems, and you will really have to work to win over this man. He will be very difficult to overcome."

I was quite interested in Dana's results with I-Ching. I had been told exactly the opposite by the persons who had arranged the appointment for me—i.e., that the meeting would present no problems and that all would go smoothly.

The appointment was for a Friday afternoon, and I was kept waiting for three-quarters of an hour before being ushered into the executive's office. Once there, Dana's predictions were realized; the man was, in fact, most difficult to please.

"Well, what do you do?" he asked. "Can you tell me how many cigarettes I have in my vest pocket? Or how many bills I have in my wallet and what their denominations are?"

"That is not the kind of work I do," I answered. "What you're asking for is a gimmick, a parlor game or a stunt performed by a stage magician."

"Well, if you don't do that, just what is it that you *can* do?"

"I can tell you the reason, for instance, why you kept me waiting for almost an hour."

He seemed interested in this statement as an opportunity to disprove my claims to being psychic. Smiling with anticipation, he said, "Ah, very good. Tell me."

"You've just come from a meeting with several people, in which you discussed a certain television project that is about to go into production. You've been made aware that the project may not go as well as planned because of the inadequacies of one of the persons in charge of it, and you were discussing whether or not to get rid of this person. Some of those in the meeting were in favor of replacing him, but others were opposed. You yourself are inclined to take this man off the project in question, but you listened carefully to the arguments against doing so. You were aware that some of those who were against replacing him took that position only because they were afraid that if they voted against him and failed to oust him, then that person might find out who his enemies were and make them pay in some way for opposing him. And that is the reason why you were late for this appointment with me."

The man didn't speak for a moment, but I could easily see that he was having a difficult time retaining his "cool." Finally he admitted, "That's close enough to what was going on in there. Tell me some more."

I had met him at five forty-five in the afternoon, and I didn't leave until almost eight o'clock. Although he was apparently impressed by my abilities, it was obvious that he still wanted me to come across with the more "spectacular"—i.e., the more marketable—kind of psychic act, the tricks and mind reading. He insisted, for example, that I choose the winners in the next day's horse races. I tried to explain that I felt my gift would not work in a situation of chance, but he insisted that this was simply another "test." Hesitantly I picked a few names from the racing form. To this day I don't know whether the horses that I picked won or lost, and I don't care to know.

The television show, in any case, is still pending.

The meeting went exactly as Dana Hutchenson had said it would. The only conclusion I can draw is either that I-Ching really works, or that Dana has a very well-developed psychic sense. And I am much more inclined to the latter than to the former.

Valerie Schwartz, the famous interior designer who helped me decorate my apartment (and became a friend in the process), had an astonishing psychic experience. She was a close friend of Paula Strasberg, wife of the eminent theatrical teacher and founder of Actors Studio, Lee Strasberg. When Mrs. Strasberg died, Valerie did not attend any of the obsequies, since she felt that it would be too upsetting. The evening of the day on which Mrs. Strasberg died was naturally an uneasy time for Valerie, and she was for many hours unable to sleep. Finally, she dozed off, and she had a vivid dream of Mrs. Strasberg's funeral. In the dream, she saw Mrs. Strasberg in her coffin, and the experience was so realistic that, on awakening, she was able to remember in its smallest detail the dress that Mrs. Strasberg had been wearing.

The following day, Valerie related her dream in its entirety to Susan Strasberg, the daughter of Paula and Lee Strasberg, and she described the dress in which she had seen Mrs. Strasberg being buried. Susan was astounded. Her mother, she said, had been placed in the coffin in exactly the same dress that Valerie described. It was a dress that no one had seen before except Susan and one other person, and neither one of them had been in touch with Valerie.

The only possible conclusion is that Valerie, because of her close friendship with Mrs. Strasberg, was subconsciously "tuned in" to the latter's vibrations. When her conscious mind "turned off" by going to sleep, these vibrations came to the fore and psychically reproduced the dream images that Valerie had seen.

Such psychic impressions often come quite quickly and unexpectedly. In August of 1967, for example, I was entertaining a Japanese house guest who expressed a desire to see Greenwich Village. We planned to go to the Village on the following Saturday evening. During the afternoon of that day, I was talking to my mother on the telephone and happened to mention that I was going to take Hyato, my guest, to Greenwich Village that evening.

"Oh, no, you mustn't go there tonight. There'll be a shooting," she said, quite out of the blue.

"Now, Mother, what on earth makes you say that?"

"I don't know," she said. "I just felt it. But with all of the violence that goes on in the city, you can never tell."

My feeling was that my mother was merely indulging herself in the sort of nervous outburst to which she is sometimes prone. She had never given any evidence of possessing an active psychic sense.

That evening, Hyato and I went to the Village as planned. We were sitting at an outdoor cafe when I heard three loud bangs directly behind me. I thought at first that they were backfires from an automobile, but Hyato, who was facing the direction from which they came, suddenly jumped up from his chair. I turned quickly, and I saw people falling flat on the sidewalk.

A car had driven down the crowded street, and a "sniper" in it had fired point-blank into the crowd, hitting one man and shattering several store windows only about forty or fifty feet from where we were sitting. It was that danger that my mother had sensed psychically.

Even animals possess a rudimentary psychic sense. They

seem to exercise it, in their own way, much more on a day-to-day basis than do humans—possibly because they are not "blocked" or inhibited by the intellectual endowment with which humans are blessed. At the present time, for instance, I have a Chihuahua named Bambi. Bambi is always aware of when I am coming home. Friends, relatives, and my secretary—any or all of whom are liable to be in my home while I am away—tell me that Bambi goes to the door about five minutes before I come home and sits there emitting a low whine. My hours are not regular—in fact, they are most irregular—but somehow, through a primitive precognitive sense, Bambi knows when I am about a block from home. This is, I understand, an extremely common phenomenon, frequently observed by people who own dogs and cats or other relatively intelligent animals.

Similarly, it can often be observed that there exists a perhaps psychic awareness between a dog and its owner which goes beyond the bounds of mere habit. While I was living in Hartford, Connecticut, for example, a woman neighbor was rushed to the hospital one night and died there of a heart attack. Her dog was found dead the next morning of a heart attack, although he had had no heart trouble before. And it is not likely that the dog's death was caused by his mistress' absence, for the lady quite regularly stayed at a friend's house overnight, leaving the dog alone at home.

Many people have had firsthand experiences with animals who sense the death of a beloved master, even when they are separated by long distances. Many such instances occur in time of war, and it happens that the animal—usually a dog—reacts violently to a psychic stimulus, howling, whining, and generally giving every evidence of knowing, long before his master's human relatives receive the news in the normal way, of the death.

One could go on and on describing the psychic experiences of persons (and animals) who are "not psychic." The multiplicity and variety of such experiences prove to me, at least, that every relatively intelligent being possesses psychic ability. And this ability is one which, when cultivated, can manifest itself in extraordinary ways for the benefit of mankind in general and of the individual in particular. When humanity finally emerges from the Middle Ages altogether, when he stops connecting psychic forces with "the work of the Devil" or with some unknown, unmentionable force, then he will emerge into the New Age of enlightenment.

11

One sign that there is an awakening in the psychic sciences abroad in the land is the success of lectures on almost any aspect of extrasensory perception. For the psychic, lecturing is one of the most rewarding as well as one of the most challenging activities in which he can engage. It is rewarding because it makes him feel that he is not operating in a vacuum, that there are indeed people who, even though they often are not "believers" in psychic phenomena in the strict sense of the term, are still interested and open-minded enough to want to have information on the subject. And it is challenging because every lecture that I give ends with a question-and-answer period in which I am forced to articulate my own beliefs and my own philosophy of life—and very often it is only by being put "on the spot" that one musters up the intellectual energy necessary to formulate one's beliefs.

The answers to the questions most commonly asked at these lectures summarize rather accurately my complex of beliefs about myself and about psychic phenomena, and it may be useful therefore to reproduce some of these here. They are representative of the queries that are raised at lectures that I have given to groups numbering no more than ten people and to audiences numbering in the thousands at Carnegie Hall and Town Hall in New York City.

QUESTION: Do you believe in spirits or ghosts? Is this where your psychic impressions come from?

ANSWER: I do not believe in what are commonly known as "ghosts" and "spirits"—that is, in souls of the dead who roam about haunting people. But I must add quickly that I do believe that, somehow, something of a person survives after death, even if only in the form of recognizable "waves" or "vibrations" in the atmosphere. I have seen too much evidence of this to allow me to believe otherwise. At times, as a medium, I am able to make contact with whatever it is that does survive. In those cases, I can only conclude that the psychic impressions that I receive must come from somewhere—but whether they come from "souls" of the departed, or from the one Creative Mind, I don't pretend to know. My own personal belief—for which I have no proof other than my experiences—is that the information that I receive and pass on concerning one's problems, questions, and one's future, come to me from a source quite different from life as we know it. For want of a more accurate designation, I call that source "the higher forces." In brief, then, I believe that information comes to me from outside of myself, from a connection with a higher force other than myself. And I further believe that this is not an accident or a quirk peculiar to me and to a few other psychics, but that everyone can establish such a connection. I think that the only difference between me and most other people is that I accept the fact that I am psychic, and my complete trust and belief in my gift has made it stronger and has developed it. I certainly do not regard myself as having been "chosen," nor do I think that I am any better or worse, morally or otherwise, than most other people. And certainly I am not more religious than they.

As I said, I cannot "prove" that there is another plane of existence where these "higher forces" dwell. The only way that I could prove it would be if I had been there. But I feel very strongly—and you might describe it as "faith"—that there are forces that are able to communicate to us whatever information we need to make a better life for ourselves, or at least to make us understand why there must be pain and suffering in life as well as joy and happiness.

QUESTION: Do you believe in reincarnation?

ANSWER: Up until a few years ago, my answer would have been an unequivocal "No." Now, however, I am more prone to admit the possibility of reincarnation. I do not have any evidence, of course, any more than Christians, Moslems, and Jews have "evidence" that there is a Heaven or a Hell. I accept it as a possibility that the "soul" can be reincarnated because it is a hypothesis that seems to explain a good deal that is mysterious about human life. For example, science has never been able to explain the fact of genius—and by "genius" I mean to say extraordinary gifts in the arts and sciences. It therefore seems reasonable to me to say that these gifts may have been carried over by the individual from another existence. And it seems particularly reasonable when dealing with an infant prodigy such as, let us say, Mozart—who was composing great music when he was still practically a baby. In addition, such stories as that of Bridey Murphy and of other, less publicized persons, cannot be, or at least have not been, explained by our sciences, but are understandable only within the context of reincarnation.

Anywhere from one-half to three-quarters of the world's population believe in reincarnation. The people of the West, however, generally reject such belief, for ours is a material, rather than a philosophical or metaphysical culture, and we are not able, without a great deal of difficulty, to grasp the concepts involved. It seems to me, however, that it is the height of irrationality to reject an idea simply because we do not understand it. It is most unscientific of a culture that prides itself, above all, on its "science."

In my own case, a belief in the possibility of reincarnation is strengthened by the circumstances of my life. As a child, I developed a great love for the Japanese people—at a time when this was looked upon as the equivalent of treason. Although I never even saw an Oriental until I was in my teens, long before that I was collecting books about the Japanese way of life, compiling scrapbooks on the subject, and secretly, in my own amateurish way, trying to live according to the ideals of Japanese culture. More recently, I feel that I can almost remember things that may have occurred in another life, in an earlier life as a Japanese. In any case, I have been told by my teachers that I have grasped the language with amazing rapidity (and I was never a brilliant student in my school days), and I am assured by Japanese friends that I am thoroughly at home with the "incomprehensible" patterns of thought of the inscrutable Japanese. To my way of thinking, a belief in reincarnation offers an explanation for this phenomenon, while the traditional religious beliefs of the West do not.

In the same way, a belief in the laws of *karma*—that is, a belief that one brings debts into the world at birth, from another existence, and that in the present life one has the opportunity to pay those debts—seems to me to offer a more reasonable explanation of why we are here than do the theories of the orthodox religions of the West.

I have seen people become absolutely enamored with a certain period of history. And I have seen collectors who would rather die than give up a unique piece dating from a period in which they are especially interested. Are such people perhaps attached to these objects because of a previous association with them in an earlier life? Is it possible that such objects provide a consoling, if unconscious, recollection of another life in another time? I do not know, for the evidence is too slight to be able to make a sound judgment. But I do know that there is no evidence at all to the contrary.

Science has very recently begun to interest itself in reincarnation. Two famous New York psychiatrists are working with the theory of reincarnation and *karma* as a possible solution to the mental problems of their patients. In fact, I have been approached by one of these psychiatrists with a request that I help him in a new field of scientific endeavor which he calls "spiritual psychiatry."

A test has already been devised by scientists that will pave the way for more investigation of the whole subject of reincarnation. In this test, a planarian worm is placed in a complicated maze. In the center of the maze is food for the worm. The worm is then prodded and pushed until it reaches the food. This is done over and over again until the worm can find its way to the center of the maze without outside help. At that point, the worm is chopped into small pieces and fed to a second worm. This second worm, when introduced into the same maze, invariably is able to head directly to the center of the maze without guidance or assistance. He has somehow absorbed the reflexes or secondary instinctual knowledge of the first worm. The conclusion seems to be that, in certain forms of life, acquired knowledge can be transmitted from one being to another along with purely material substance—an important factor in the study of reincarnation.

If I have gone on at length in answer to the original question, it is because reincarnation is a vast subject—as vast and as complex as any of the major theological and philosophical problems that have occupied the minds of Occidental thinkers in centuries past. It is a subject that is too important and too far-reaching in its implications for it to continue to be ignored by Americans.

QUESTION: You mentioned that you sometimes go into a trance. What exactly is a trance? Do these "higher forces" enter your body? Do outside entities actually take over your being, your personality, or do you feel that you remain yourself when you are in a trance?

ANSWER: A trance is, in its simplest definition, simply a state of sleep, not unlike the "nervous sleep" of hypnosis; that is, it is a sleep in which certain faculties of the medium are heightened while others (particularly those normally controlled by the conscious mind) become dormant. In a trance, as in hypnosis, the medium's condition is characterized by physical lethargy, by immobility and plasticity of attitude, and by alert intelligence and definite personality. And the medium, as in the case of a hypnotic subject, is "passive" in the sense that he is the "receiver" through which vibrations are received. In many respects, then, trance is identical with the hypnotic state. In fact, some authorities maintain that there is no essential difference between trance and hypnosis.

As to whether the "higher forces" actually enter my body and take it over, I cannot honestly say for certain because the medium does not normally remember what happens while he is in a trance. I do know that while I am in trance my voice actually changes and its tone, inflections, and even its vocabulary are different from mine. I have heard tape recordings of my trance sessions, and I feel certain that it was not completely Daniel Logan who was speaking. Most of the things that I have said while in trance are things that I myself have never even thought about.

QUESTION: If you really possess the gift that you claim, why is it that you aren't a millionaire? Can't you use your gift to make a fortune on the stock market or at the racetrack?

ANSWER: The reason that I am not a millionaire is that, generally speaking, a medium is not able to use his gift for his own benefit in general; and it seems that this specific point is one in which he is not able to use it at all. Once or twice I have invested money on the basis of psychic impressions—and on each occasion it turned out that I was completely wrong. One time I had a very strong impression that a forthcoming Broadway production would be a tremendous success, and so I invested quite heavily in it. A few nights before the show was supposed to open, the star who had the lead role suddenly became ill—and I lost my entire investment.

It is remarkable that whenever a medium tries to use his gift for monetary gain or for other selfish purposes, the gift fails. This has been proved true not only in my own case, but in that of many famous mediums (Edgar Cayce, for example), some of whom I have known. It seems that it is only when the psychic's intention is to help others or enlighten them that the gift is operational.

QUESTION: Does that mean that you can't use your gift to help yourself in any way at all in your own life, with your own problems?

ANSWER: Well, yes and no. I am so close to my own problems that it is usually not possible to use the gift in solving them. Remember, it is necessary for me to "turn off" myself before I can begin to receive psychic impressions during a reading—and I have yet to discover how to turn myself off and at the same time think about my own problems. On the other hand, it happens sometimes that I receive impressions about my own life while I am thinking about someone else's problems, or while in deep meditation or trance.

It would be very difficult for me to try to explain why it is that the medium so often is the only one who cannot benefit from his gift. Probably the most reasonable explanation is that it is a disposition of Providence, intended to point out that, beyond the shadow of a doubt, a psychic gift is intended to be used for the benefit of others rather than for the psychic's own selfish ends.

QUESTION: If a psychic sees that a certain event will take place in the future, does this mean that that event must necessarily take place and that nothing can be done to change it? For example, when Jeane Dixon predicted that President Kennedy would be assassinated while in office, did that mean that the event had already, in a sense, taken place in the future and that it would have been impossible to avoid it? If President Kennedy had believed Mrs. Dixon's prediction and had—by a far stretch of imagination—barricaded himself within the White House and seen only his family and closest associates, would the assassination necessarily have taken place?

The second part of the question is this: If a predicted event cannot in fact be avoided, then of what use is a psychic's "guidance"?

ANSWER: That is a complicated question, and requires a complicated answer. The fact is, it is not the function of the psychic to change the course of events for the benefit of an individual; indeed, it is not in his power to do so even if he wished to. All that a psychic can do is to point out certain difficulties and problems that he feels will arise in a person's life, or to warn someone of approaching danger. The psychic is quite simply—if you will allow me to use this simile—like the one literate person in a community of illiterates. He can read books to the people around him, but he cannot change what is in the books.

The benefit of a consultation is that the psychic can do two things for a client. First, he can prepare the client for a situation that is in the future. For instance, if I foresee a sudden death in a client's immediate family, in most cases the client is better able to accept the event when it occurs because the element of surprise and shock has been removed to a considerable extent. In such a case, however, the psychic simply foresees the fact, and there is nothing that he can do to prevent its occurrence.

The second thing that a psychic is able to do for a client is contingent on the fact that much of what he foresees is dependent on circumstances for its fulfillment. I mean by that that there is often a big IF somewhere in the prediction. For example, I was once told by a friend that *if* I left the city during the month of August, I would miss out on a valuable opportunity on television. I heeded her warning, and I did not accept the out-of-town engagements that were offered during that month—and I was invited to appear on a television show. Now, if I had not been warned, then I would very likely have left the city during August and missed that opportunity. So, the psychic, in addition to being able to prepare someone to meet a problem, is often able to see the outcome of a certain set of circumstances or conditions; and, in the latter case, the person who has consulted the medium is able to make an alternate choice, as I did, to protect himself from one situation and to take advantage of another.

Now, in the Kennedy case, Jeane Dixon sensed psychically that President Kennedy would be assassinated because she sensed what his choice would be; that is, that he would choose to go into the danger area which, in this case, was Dallas. So, the element of chance or circumstance in this instance was largely removed. Mrs. Dixon did not say "the President may be killed." She said "he will be killed." In other words, she was positive because she saw the choice as well as its consequence.

It should be said, too, that sometimes the vibrations change in a particular situation; and that is why people come back more than once for a consultation. The most accurate and most detailed psychic advice can be given over an extended period of time—just as medical advice based on a thorough physical examination is liable to be more accurate than when based on a cursory examination.

During the course of my lectures and of the question-and-answer periods I have often noticed that my audience is somewhat shocked when I mention that I am sometimes wrong in my predictions. No one seems to expect a doctor, or an architect, or an engineer, or a carpenter to be infallible; but the poor medium apparently is required to be completely on target at all times. Unfortunately the psychic medium is only a human being dealing with human situations; the flesh is weak, and the situations are variable. To me, it seems that if the psychic gives evidence of a reasonable percentage of accuracy then he has done something quite extraordinary. Given the circumstances in which a psychic works and the material with which he deals, it seems to me remarkable that I am able to maintain an accuracy of eighty percent. But the attitude of the public often is not that I am right eighty percent of the time, but that I am wrong twenty percent of the time.

Occasionally, however, one understanding soul presents itself and makes one believe that all is not wrong with the world. One such instance occurred while I was preparing to tape my television special for David Susskind. Everyone in the Susskind office was eager for me to tell them what was in the future for them—everyone, that is, except one young lady. After a while, I became curious at her apparent lack of interest and asked her why she alone of everyone in the office had not approached me for an impromptu reading.

"Daniel," she said, "I don't want to 'bug' you the way most of them seem to be doing, because I'm not interested in checking your accuracy. That you can predict accurately even one or two things out of ten would be more than enough proof for me that you have a gift. Everyone is watching you to see if you were wrong in the predictions you made about their lives, and if you were wrong even in one case they'll come back and say, 'Aha, he was wrong.' But, in the meantime, they themselves can't make one single prediction. As for me, it's evidence enough for me if a single one of your predictions come true."

"Like apples of gold in a silver setting," says the Book of Proverbs, "is the word that is aptly spoken."

12

On Friday nights during 1965, 1966, and 1967 I presided over small group meetings in New York. The group usually comprised only ten or eleven "regulars," and was occasionally augmented by one or two guests. The meetings were actually trance sessions and were held for the benefit of people interested in spiritual enlightenment and in the development of their psychic sense.

During these sessions, I went into a deep trance state, very much like that described earlier on the occasion of Deon Frey's seance. Unlike my early trances, however, the only unpleasant aftereffect that I suffered was a feeling of complete exhaustion which sometimes endured for two days. (Finally, because of this depletion, and because of overwork in private consultations, I had to bring a halt to the meetings in the fall of 1967.)

The method I employed to induce trance was simple and similar to that described before. I lay on a sofa, sometimes in darkness and sometimes with a single candle burning. After a short meditation, I would drift off into trance, and a feeling of disembodiment would come over me. I felt as though I were free of physical limits. A few more minutes passed, and then a voice spoke through my mouth. It was not my voice, but a high-pitched voice that spoke in a vaguely central-European accent. At some of the meetings, more than one voice spoke through me. The voice, or voices, offered personal advice to those present and, occasionally, discoursed on world conditions.

Those who attended these sessions were not, generally speaking, sensation-seekers or, at the other end of the spectrum, unbalanced fanatics of the kind that infest ordinary psychic convocations. Those present had been carefully screened, and I was satisfied that they were intelligent, serious people with a serious interest in psychic phenomena. Each of them, naturally, had different problems and different needs, and it was because of those problems and needs that they had sought me out after having heard of me by virtue of my television appearances or lectures.

One of those present was Valerie Benjker, of Brooklyn. With a friend, Elizabeth Cummings, Valerie had happened to attend a lecture at the Philosophical Society of New York where I had appeared many times. The two ladies had come in search of guidance and consolation, as they had recently lost a third friend who had been part of an intimate circle of women. Both Valerie and Elizabeth were interested in metaphysics and had studied it for many years. At the end of the lecture, when I usually give impressions to individuals in the audience, I singled out Valerie.

"I sense a recent death," I said. "You have lost a very close friend, and her death is very much in your mind. I sense that you took care of your friend during her last illness, which was caused by a heart condition. You must not mourn for your friend, however, because the vibrations I sense now are happy ones."

Since it was virtually impossible for me to have known about her friend through purely sensory means, Valerie was quite shaken by what I said. She waited for me after the meeting, and said, "I don't know how you knew about this, but it is certainly true. We have lost a very close friend who died of a heart ailment only a week ago, and I took care of her during her illness."

We talked for a while, and before leaving Valerie asked if there was any way in which they could learn more about my gift. On the basis of our conversation, it was evident that the two ladies' interest was centered around the possibility of growing in an understanding of man's spiritual nature. I therefore invited them to attend the Friday night meetings.

On the night of the first meeting that they attended I went into a deep trance as usual. After a time, the voice addressed Valerie.

"You should know," it said, "that there is much gratitude for the love, kindness, and help you gave to your friend who has passed away."

"Do you mean that our friend is trying to thank us?" Valerie asked.

"That is correct."

"But that means," Valerie continued, "that she continues to exist somewhere. How can we believe this?"

The voice did not give a direct answer to her question, but seemed to suggest proof that something of Valerie's friend had survived. "I should like to recall to you a gift that you once gave your friend. Do you remember that when she first became a part of your circle of friends she shortly went on a trip? And when she returned you gave her a bouquet of flowers as a coming-home present. The flowers happened to be her favorite, which you did not know at the time, and she was most grateful for your thoughtfulness."

"That's true. I remember that. But can you tell what kind of flowers they were?" Valerie was not demanding proof. Rather, she was so astonished at the details of the long-forgotten incident that she was eager to see how much more she might receive.

"Yes," the voice answered. "The flowers were violets."

"My God," Valerie exclaimed. "She must be present in some form. No one knew about this bouquet of flowers except the two of us—and even that was many years ago."

In a subsequent meeting, the voice described in abundant detail a certain walk near the home of the dead woman. Everything that one would pass while strolling on the walk was described by the voice, even to certain rocks.

In private consultation at about the same time, I told Valerie that she would soon have to care for her other friend, Elizabeth Cummings, who would become ill in the near future. This was very difficult for Valerie to accept. Unfortunately, however, I have just received, as I am writing this, the news that Miss Cummings has been taken ill, and that two operations will be necessary. Valerie, of course, intends to care for her friend during her illness.

Valerie is an intelligent and inquiring woman, and she has made many attempts to resolve to her satisfaction the question of how my gift works; but she has thus far been unsuccessful. Now, she is content to conclude that it is mystical in nature—that is, that she must accept it because she has seen it in operation, but that it is not necessary for her to understand it.

One of the most practical and detailed courses of action that the voice laid out was given for the guidance of Miss Jean D'Dominico, a consultant for the New York School for the Deaf. For a long time at several sessions, and over a long period of time, the voice gave to Jean advice that seemed to the others present to be vague and rather meaningless, and Jean's questions to the voice were equally mysterious. The fact was that she was being advised on the buying of property and the building of a home, and Jean had not wanted anyone to know of it until the project had been completed. As it turned out, the voice had guided her through every detail of purchase, location, construction, legal complications—and even given advice on how to rid the area of mice!

On several occasions, the voice had also warned Jean to be careful with her new car. There seemed to be some unexpected and unspecified danger involved. A few weeks later, the car was recalled by the manufacturer as being one of a group from which certain parts had inadvertently been omitted.

Another "regular" at these meetings was Bill Murray, an actor who originally came to New York from the Midwest. Bill, in order to supplement his theatrical income, had been working as a waiter at the famous discothèque Arthur. On one occasion, the voice warned Bill of impending danger in the next few weeks. (Bill himself had already received the impression that Arthur would be wrecked, and another waiter there had had the same premonition in a dream.) A short time later, a brawl broke out at the discothèque, during the course of which the place was wrecked and several people were seriously injured.

On another occasion, Bill was told that a lady would shortly come into his life, and that she would be instrumental in his going to California. As had been predicted, Bill did meet such a lady.

Nadia Loftus, of New York City, was told that she would be successful in selling a group of paintings of which she was trying to dispose. The voice, while informing Nadia of this, made an apparently irrelevant reference to roses. As it happened, however, the paintings comprised the entire collection of rose paintings by Adolf Müller-Ury.

Esther Wiland, also of New York, was directed to a doctor other than the one she had been consultating for the relief of a hearing difficulty. Upon taking this advice, she improved enormously.

Perhaps the most bizarre phenomenon that took place during these trance sessions was the occurrence of an *apport*. (An *apport*—the word itself is from the French, meaning a "carrying in"—is the penetration of an object into a closed space, such as a room, by other than natural means.) Up until that time, I confess that I had always been skeptical of *apports*. It had too often been proved that *apports* had been faked by mediums who hid the object to be materialized on their persons or elsewhere in the room until the auspicious moment. On the other hand, in the case of such renowned and unimpeachable mediums as Helene Smith, *apports* are said to have materialized under the strictest (and most skeptical) scientific scrutiny. Whatever the case, I mention my own case of *apport* here to explain the experience of Miss Devera Levin at one of my group meetings.

The voice was speaking to Devera of various personal matters of consequence only to her when it suddenly interrupted itself and warned her "not to be afraid." In the next instant, Devera was struck on the arm by something that seemed to be flying through the air. It was a half-used spool of thread.

"This spool of thread," the voice said, "belonged to the dead mother of the friend who recently visited you from the Midwest. It is brought to you as a sign, as proof."

Devera is an intelligent and determined young lady who is quite taken with parapsychology. But she can be mercilessly skeptical of things that seem to pass the bounds of credibility. After the trance, I could see that she was more angry at having been struck so hard than she was impressed at being the recipient of an *apport*.

The next week, Devera told me that she had telephoned her friend in the Midwest. She had learned that the friend's mother, when alive, had done quite a bit of sewing. "In fact," said the friend, "at the time of her death she had been working on a dark brown suit."

The spool of half-used thread that had struck Devera was dark brown.

At the time of the *apport*, some members of the group felt the materialization could have been faked. Most certainly it was not faked—but it is certainly possible that it could have been. However, there could have been no way to know the color of the thread that the friend's mother had been using at the time of her death.

If the incident of the *apport* was a most unusual happening at the trance sessions, the most troublesome one undoubtedly was a prediction concerning the Kennedy family. One evening in the spring of 1965, a dark, impassioned voice, quite different from the usual high-pitched one, emanated from my mouth. "Jacqueline . . . Jacqueline . . . Jacqueline," it repeated over and over again.

No one in the room was named Jacqueline, and no one answered.

"Jacqueline, where are you?" the voice pleaded.

Finally, Clara Hoover, whose apartment had been used for many of the trance sessions, spoke up. "What is it that you want?"

"I want to say . . . to tell Jacqueline . . ." the voice began, then trailed off.

"There is no Jacqueline here," pointed out Eleanor Butterworth, another member of the group. "Tell us what it is you want to say."

The voice spoke sadly, in broken phrases. "Where ... tell her ... the children ... it's dangerous ... don't let them go on the boat ... it's not good ..."

It made little sense, and the group was thus far frustrated in its efforts to find out what it all meant.

"Can you mean Jacqueline Kennedy?" William McCarthy ventured.

"Kennedy ... Kennedy ..." the voice repeated. "Tell Jacqueline she must not ... must not go ... on the yacht. Someone ... will ... drown. Danger ... John-John ... she must not ... take the children ..."

As unexpectedly as it had come the voice now disappeared. On the following Friday, however, it spoke again, and more clearly this time, with the same message. "Tell Jacqueline that she must not go on the yacht. Someone will drown. There is danger. She must not take the children."

Apparently the late President's family would be in danger if they boarded a yacht. That was the substance of the message. "Tell Jacqueline," the voice had directed. But how does one go about telling the former First Lady of a warning received from an unidentified voice during a psychic trance? We discussed what was to be done and decided that we were bound to do our best to deliver the message somehow.

The first thing that occurred to me was to write to Mrs. Kennedy. But I quickly discarded that idea because of the likelihood that any such letter would be "screened out" by a battery of secretaries. I decided instead to attempt to telephone Mrs. Kennedy at the New York office which the government had placed at her disposal. I did so, and was told by a secretary to call the Kennedy summer home at Hyannisport and to leave the meassage there. I did call, as she suggested, but I simply left my name, address, and telephone number, and stated that I had a message which concerned the well-being of the Kennedy family. I knew that would get a response of some kind. It did. In a very short time, the New York City office of the Secret Service called me and asked for an appointment.

We met in the Park Avenue apartment of Miss Clara Hoover. (I had asked Miss Hoover for the use of her apartment because I felt that the message would be taken more seriously if it was delivered in surroundings not usually associated with "crank messages.") There were two Secret Service men, one in his fifties and the other apparently in his twenties. The pair could have been sent by Central Casting in Hollywood so completely did they fit the stereotyped image of plain-clothes cops the world over—an uneasy overcompensatingly brusque manner, nervous glances around the room. Despite the seriousness of the occasion, I could not help smiling at their obviousness. At the same time, I knew that they were not sensitive, intellectual types who would be willing to admit the possibility of things beyond their understanding. It was going to be rough and I had begun to regret having started the whole thing. But it was too late for regrets now.

The older of the two took out a notebook and started questioning me: name, credentials, and other personal data. Then he asked, "Now, what exactly is this information you have concerning the safety of the Kennedy family?"

"I think this information should be passed directly to the Kennedys themselves, or to someone close to them," I said.

"That's impossible," the man said. "You can be sure that if it's at all worth while, if it makes any sense at all, we'll see that the Kennedys get it."

"But my psychic sense tells me that you have no intention of passing on this information to Mrs. Kennedy or to anyone around her."

The man hemmed and hawed a bit, but finally admitted, "Well, to tell you the truth, we get quite a few people who have had so-called dreams and premonitions about the Kennedys."

"I'm sure you must," I answered. "And if you had listened to at least one of them, Jeane Dixon, President Kennedy might be alive today."

The older man's face turned red. "Listen," he said, "if we had taken as fact all the so-called psychic predictions of death we received about President Kennedy he never would have been able to go outside of the White House."

"But Jeane Dixon is a well-respected clairvoyant with a

long record of accuracy, not a fanatic or a nut. And yet she wasn't taken seriously."

There was no reply.

"Listen," said the younger man. "Tell us your story. I've been with Mrs. Kennedy many times, and I promise to pass on your information to the proper people if it warrants it."

I could see there was no way to get around these men, and that the only way to get to Mrs. Kennedy was through them—however slim the chance might be that the message would eventually reach her.

"During one of my trance sessions," I said, "a voice came, and it warned a person, whom it called 'Jacqueline,' of a drowning. It mentioned the children."

"Do you actually believe this voice was that of the late President?" one of the men asked incredulously.

"I didn't say that," I answered. "I really don't know. It was a strange voice, almost incoherent at times; and it spoke in unfinished sentences."

"What else did this 'voice' say to you?" The older man had stopped taking notes—an unmistakable sign that he felt the story to be so much nonsense.

"The voice said something about a boat, a yacht, and it seemed concerned that the Kennedys not go aboard."

At that, the men seemed startled. "What do you know about a boat?" the older one demanded.

"Just what the voice said. It seemed to be warning of a yacht, and it said there would be a drowning."

"A yacht? Whose yacht? Who would drown? The children? Mrs. Kennedy?"

"I don't know. The voice didn't say who would drown. But it did seem to be more concerned with the children."

I had the impression that the men felt I knew something more about the boat than I was telling, and they asked me a number of rather clumsy questions with the perfectly obvious intention of trapping me into an admission that I had not told them everything. It was nonsense, of course. I had told them everything that I knew.

Finally, after having reassured me once again that they would do what they could, the Secret Service men left.

The sequel to this incident did not take place until the summer months. At the time, a widely reproduced photgraph appeared in most of the newspapers of the country. It purported to be a photograph of Mrs. Kennedy boarding Frank Sinatra's yacht for a vacation trip. A few days later, Mrs. Kennedy's office issued a statement to the effect that the lady in the photograph was not Mrs. Kennedy herself but her secretary—who, they said, happened to look like Mrs. Kennedy. (At that time, of course, Mrs. Kennedy had to be most discreet in her public appearances. It seemed that the country was filled with self-appointed guardians of propriety who felt that they should be the judges of when it was time for Mrs. Kennedy to come out of mourning.)

On that occasion, one of the crewmen of Sinatra's yacht fell into the water and was drowned while he was being towed in a rowboat. It is possible that it was this incident about which the voice had attempted to warn Mrs. Kennedy. If Mrs. Kennedy had taken the children aboard the yacht, it is possible that the children would have been in the rowboat and that they also would have drowned. Or was the voice merely trying to protect Mrs. Kennedy from the resulting publicity had she been on board when the man was drowned? Indeed, was the photograph one of Mrs. Kennedy or of her secretary? I do not know. Perhaps the two men from the Secret Service do.

This encounter with the Secret Service was the only occasion on which I have had contact, as a psychic, with a government agency. And, if I have anything to say about it, it will be the last time. Although I have been asked to render assistance in several homicide cases and other police work, I have politely declined. Once was enough. Besides, I don't feel that it is a psychic's job to play detective.

Many of these trance sessions were held in the home of Miss Clara Hoover, and the extensive trance work that I did on her behalf will be described in detail in the next chapter. It will suffice here to say that Miss Hoover received guidance in many areas of her life. In one such incident, the voice informed Miss Hoover that the attorneys whom she had retained to straighten out a legal problem were not the right men for the job and that she must change lawyers if she wished to have the problem resolved properly. The voice then spelled out the name

MacDonald, and gave an address in the 400 block of Park Avenue. It turned out that there was an attorney named Charles MacDonald in the 400 block of Park Avenue; the address the voice had given was off by one digit. Mr. MacDonald took Miss Hoover's legal affairs in hand and he has given her satisfaction. Although the attorneys whom she had first retained were regarded as top men in their specialty, it was not until Miss Hoover turned her affairs over to Mr. MacDonald that her problems were solved.

I rarely perform trance work outside of such private meetings as the ones I have described. For one thing, it is difficult to find the right people for this form of psychic operation; those who want to attend most often are either skeptics who regard it as a "test" of some sort, or they are lightheaded people looking for amusement who regard the whole thing as some sort of fascinating, though interesting, parlor game.

Occasionally, however, I make exceptions, and once I undertook trance work for Jean Avery, a model and actress, and her three children. The children had been brought up in an environment wholly sympathetic to spiritual teachings and understanding, and I gave each of them a private trance-reading. The session with the seven-year-old son of Miss Avery was the most interesting of the three. His complete understanding of everything that was taking place was amazing, and it is an experience simply to listen to the tape of his conversation with the voice. He was told what his likes and dislikes were, what kind of work he would go into as an adult, and when he would attain success, and the boy's response was one of quiet acknowledgment in matters of fact and equally quiet acquiescence in matters of the future.

In the session for Miss Avery herself, the voice asked whether she knew a man named Stanley. Miss Avery answered that she did, that Stanley was a former boy friend about whom she had been quite serious at one time.

"There seems to be a Marilyn connected with this man," the voice told her. "Do you understand?"

"Yes, I understand," Jean said.

"There is also something about a fire."

"Yes," she said, this time with a hint of sadness.

Miss Avery told me later that "Stanley" had been Marilyn Monroe's first manager, and that he had died in a fire (once more a connection with Marilyn Monroe).

The voice told Miss Avery's elder daughter that the next acting job that came into the family would be hers, and that it would occur in the immediate future. Within a month, the girl had been signed to play the lead in a film called *The Plastic Dome of Norma Jean*—which is a story about a young girl with psychic ability who is exploited by a group of grasping people. Norma Jean was Marilyn Monroe's born name.

As I have said, most of the information that is relayed through trance work is of a personal nature, having to do with the problems and situations of those present. Occasionally, however, the voice goes on to other matters. This happened during a trance early in 1966, and it was one of those enlightening occasions when the voice spoke of world conditions. It is perhaps fitting to conclude this chapter with a verbatim transcription of a series of messages given during that trance which are of some importance to everyone concerned:

The years ahead for the United States are not pleasant ones to look forward to. The war in Vietnam will continue for at least several years yet, and it will grow in intensity. Although it may be brought to a temporary end for political reasons just before the 1968 elections, it will break out again shortly after that, if not in Vietnam itself then in another section of southern Asia. Thailand is in a most dangerous position. The Communists want this country next.

There is the strongest vibration of a major war in the 1980s. The side of the coin which reads WAR is very clear. The vibrations of the earth are at their lowest level since the earth was created. You who are spiritually minded can sense this. Those who do not grovel in the materialism in which the United States is presently steeped need no warning, for they can feel destruction in the very air they breathe.

Inflation faces your country by 1968. In the early 1970s there will be a depression in which many small businesses will fail. Strikes, rises in prices, and a shortage of employment will prevail in the United States.

Natural catastrophes, in the United States as well as in other parts of the world, will be much in evidence. The climactic changes now occurring in the world will become more noticeable. The spring and fall months will be things of the past, and the climate of earth will be one of extremes of heat and cold. The earth has been moved almost imperceptibly off its previous axis by the detonation of atomic weapons, and those which have been exploded under the surface of the earth are those that have done the most damage.

Earthquakes, long predicted by psychics, will strike not only the west coast of America but also the east coast. Many countries of the Middle East also will be devastated by earthquakes, and thousands shall die.

The value of all monies shall decrease, and even gold will be devaluated. This will occur first in England. The most secure place for money will be in Japan, which, within the next thirty years, will become the foremost industrial nation of the world. There will be a natural disaster there, but enough will survive to make of that country one of the most advanced on earth.

Nostradamus said, "In the twentieth century, the city of mirrors shall crumble with a crash." The city of mirrors is the city of New York.

Those of you who are spiritual shall be saved, you will be led away before the time comes for the destruction of the cities. In droves will you move away from those areas which have been so material that no one can exist in them unless he also is wholly material. If you do not believe, open your inner eye and see how the human race has degenerated in so short a time.

The war in Vietnam could have been brought to a conclusion long before it will. Those who are involved prolong the war for their own political or financial gain.

The space program of the United States will be delayed many times. Death in strange incidents will befall the astronauts.

The Roman Catholic Church shall rise above its misdeeds and become a leading force in the next twenty-five years. Changes and reforms will occur quickly in this new and respected leader.

Break-throughs in the cure of major illnesses will occur in the next ten to twenty years. Many forms of cancer will be found to be preventable and curable. The cause of cancer will be found to be a virus. The new danger will be in mental, rather than physical, disease.

Russia and the United States will become allies and will eventually fight against the real danger, Red China. China will be regarded as the great enemy of mankind. That country has little to lose except population, and she regards a major loss in population as desirable.

The messages the voice gave are not joyful ones, and there seems to be little hope. Indeed, the only real hope of the world seems to lie in the hands of its youth who, despite all the obstacles that the masters of corruption and greed place in their path, may yet create a world of peace and brotherhood.

13

For ordinary consultations, as I mentioned earlier, I do not go into a trance, since the "turning off" that I described is sufficient for what is required. There are times, however, when the trance state is not only useful but necessary. One such instance is when one wishes to have an oral transcription, as it were, of the vibrations in the air—as when I went into a trance during Deon Frey's psychometry session and became the instrument through which were registered the vibrations of the mother of Deon's fiancé. The trance state is particularly intriguing and interesting inasmuch as the medium usually has no control over what is said through his mouth and, in many cases, the vibrations received are not identifiable as those of this or that deceased individual.

Obviously the trance state is something that must be mastered and employed by any psychic who wishes to operate at optimum capacity. So, despite the near-catastrophe of my first attempt at trance, and encouraged by my success at Miss Frey's seance, I soon lost my fear and became adept at inducing, and operating during, trances.

The most concentrated and intensive trance work that I have ever done was undertaken at the request of Miss Clara Hoover, of New York City. Miss Hoover showed me great kindness, particularly at the beginning of my career, when I needed it most, and even gave me the use of a room in her Park Avenue apartment for my work. My gratitude to her is boundless. This series of trances, which took place from June of 1965 through 1966, I therefore refer to as "the Hoover trances."

Miss Hoover is a well-organized, accurate, and thorough person. She took endless and very detailed notes during the entire series, and it is mostly from her notes that I have extracted the following excerpts from the material of the trances. The questions were asked by Miss Hoover or by other persons who were present during the trances. (My first group meetings were held there.)

June 11, 1965

On this day, Miss Hoover had the first of many private trance sessions. On this occasion, a voice speaking through my mouth—it was not my voice, but was different in tone and quality from mine, and it was the same voice that was used throughout the entire series of trances—directed Miss Hoover to look up at the ceiling. She saw there a series of triangular forms, of different sizes and colors, which had appeared as though by projection.

The triangle, the voice said, was a symbol dating from the time of ancient Egypt and standing for spiritual truth. "The pyramids are triangular," it said, "and throughout religious history the number three plays a significant role; for example, in the doctrine of the Trinity—the Father, the Son, and the Holy Ghost."

Strangely enough, the triangles were still visible after I came out of the trance, and they continued moving across the ceiling for several minutes. Their perfection of form and the beauty of their colors is beyond description, and this particular session remains in my memory as the most beautiful visual psychic experience that I have undergone.

June 17, 1965

QUESTION: Was Edgar Cayce correct in predicting, while in trance, a vast destruction that would occur on earth and particularly in the United States?

ANSWER: Yes. By the early years of the twenty-first century, a large part of the earth will have been changed. New York City will no longer exist, and Atlantis will rise again when New York is destroyed. There will be many geographic changes, but these changes, for the most part, will bring many glorious things upon the earth. All of the materialistic beings who presently occupy the seats of power on earth will no longer exist in the twenty-first century. And, after the destruction, there will be peace, once and forever. It will be a New Age.

QUESTION: But why must New York City be destroyed?

ANSWER: Not only New York, but many of the earth's largest cities will be destroyed. And this widespread destruction will not be the result of exterior forces, but of the thinking of the people; for as a man thinketh, so he is. In any given city, events are ruled by the thoughts of its inhabitants. In New York City, the thoughts of the majority of the people are now of low vibration and are totally materialistic and unloving. To walk the streets of your city brings to mind two similar cities: Sodom and Gomorrah. And, as those cities were destroyed, so too will the materialistic cities of your time surely die. Those who are concerned only with material things will scoff and say that this is impossible; but those who seek the things of the spirit know that doom is in the very air you breathe.

QUESTION: There has been much written lately on the injustices inflicted on the American Indian by the white man. Is this one of the evils for which the people of the United States will have to suffer?

ANSWER: The Indian was upon the lands of the Americas long before the white man came. It is, in truth, his land. And when the Indian extended his hand in friendship to the white man, as he did in their first meetings, the white man repaid him by ridicule, by treating him as though he were a beast, by torturing and murdering him. The Indian has suffered and retrogressed mentally and spiritually—in every way—because of his treatment by the white man. If you feel there will be no retribution, no karma, for this great wrong, then you are mistaken.

For many thousands of years, the Indian lived upon his land. He was free. He was a powerful spiritual force, and most of the religions of the world can be traced back to the ancient ways and teachings of those whom the white man chose to regard as savages. He spent a third of each day in meditation or in communing, in some way, with forces greater than he. Spiritually he was so advanced that he was able to cure most human diseases, even cancers, and he was able to receive answers to his daily problems and needs through his faith and his trust in the Great Spirit. When the white man saw this great spiritual attainment, however, he called it the work of the Devil and forced the Indian to abandon it and take up the ways of the Christian religion. And the latter has all but destroyed the great power of the Indian.

The Indian then indeed became a savage, out of the need to protect his home and his people. He committed savage crimes, using the ways of the white man as an example. And if the whole truth were known about the ways of the white man with respect to the Indian, the word "savage" would then be better applied to the lighter-skinned of the two.

QUESTION: Is it possible to develop a psychic, or spiritual nature, or must one be born with it?

ANSWER: Do not confuse spirituality with being psychic. It is far better to be spiritual than to be psychic.

But to answer your question: Yes, it is possible to develop both one and the other. For example, Christ Jesus—who, next to Buddha, was the most spiritual man ever to walk the earth—did not simply emerge as a great spiritual leader shortly before his thirtieth year. He spent much of his early life studying with the teachers and masters of the East. There is little in the Bible about his life between his fifteenth and thirtieth years, but you may be certain that he did not simply wander from mountain to mountain gathering spiritual strength. He spent much of this time being taught by the learned ones of Africa and Egypt. And eventually this phase of Christ Jesus' life will become known through the appearance of certain writings that will come to light by virtue of a great archaeological discovery in Egypt.

Thus, Christ Jesus developed "divine consciousness" over a long period of time. So also Buddha meditated many years before he received the higher teachings. Neither of them were born with their spiritual and psychic powers fully developed. They chose to walk in the path of light, and they then worked in order to attain to a high degree of spirituality.

July 6, 1965

QUESTION: Naturally, we are most concerned with the various predictions of destruction. Can you tell us anything more about this? What of the countless innocent people who will have to suffer?

ANSWER: New York—what you really want to know about is New York—will be destroyed. The time, however, is not fixed for a certain moment. There may yet come a change in the thinking of your people which will prevent, at least for a time, the destruction. There will be warnings and signs for the innocent. There will be drought, followed by much water. Then, drought again, followed by flooding. The weather will change entirely. It will be colder in winter, always damp, and unbeara-

ble in summer. There will be neither fall nor spring.
There will be only extremes in the weather, as there are
extremes in thinking.

Again, remember, it is the thinking of the majority
that will bring this about. By the year two thousand, if
there is not a major change in the level of thinking
and action, New York will be gone. But the difficulty in
dealing with the weather, and the low level of vibrations, will force the sensitive, the spiritual ones, out of
New York City. And that is how the innocent ones will
be protected, or saved.

QUESTION: How long will the war in Southern Asia last?

ANSWER: The war in southern Asia will last for many
years, well into the 1970s. It may cease for a short
while, but it will spring up again and spread to many
sections which have not yet been affected.

QUESTION: What can we do about this?

ANSWER: It is the "big business" of the countries involved
that prevents the war from ending. In the past, the
United States was victorious in war because it was, for
the most part, in the right. The higher forces assisted
and protected your country. This war, however, is completely evil, and your country is now in the wrong. I
could have ended the Vietnam war years ago.

Therefore, the spiritual protection afforded your
country in the past has now been lifted.

July 16, 1965

QUESTION: Is there any truth of reincarnation?

ANSWER: Yes, but it will never be explained entirely to the
people of earth. If it were, there would be no reason for
reincarnation.

One comes back only as another human being, never
as a lower form of life. You have nothing to learn from
coming back as an animal. The earth is a school, and
the souls are placed here to learn. They have been

disobedient elsewhere and are under an obligation to make the right choices by making amends (karma) in their present incarnation. One meets countless souls that it has known before, and one is given the power to choose whether or not to pay the debts owed to these other souls. If the debt is paid lovingly, the karma is lifted. If the debt is unpaid, however, more karma is added onto the soul, which must be paid again in a subsequent incarnation—on earth or elsewhere.

QUESTION: What do you mean by "elsewhere"?

ANSWER: Other planets, other phases of existence. Your earth is far from final. Contrary to what most of your scientists believe, there are other planets where there is life. It is extremely egocentric of your scientific and religious leaders to teach that God would create vast numbers of planets and even of galaxies, and then restrict life to one of the smallest planets.

uly 19, 1965

QUESTION: Does sickness come from the mind, as many of the metaphysical religions teach?

ANSWER: Yes, most sicknesses are created first in the mind. There are diseases, however, which are carried over from a previous incarnation. In that case, one has the opportunity to overcome any sickness brought with one from another phase of existence.

Some of earth's metaphysical religions, nonetheless, err when they teach that a man can heal himself by means of his own thinking alone. There are on earth the minds of great doctors and thinkers; they have been placed there to be used, and one should turn to these in time of need.

There is too much self-will taught and practiced by earth's so-called metaphysicians. It is not meant that you suffer, but that you overcome suffering—and, most importantly, that you overcome your need for suffering. There is, however, no power in an individual mind, other than by virtue of its recognition of the Great Power.

QUESTION: Many of today's psychic mediums have stated that a new saviour has been born in the Middle East. Is this true?

ANSWER: To some extent, it is true. A child was indeed born in Egypt in 1962 who will be a great leader. But his coming will not be what is signified by the "Second Coming." Nonetheless, he will lead many to recognize the truth. We are working to protect him from the horror that will soon arise in the Middle East.

July 23, 1965

QUESTION: Recently, a rocket was sent to Mars and took photographs of that planet. What can you tell us about this?

ANSWER: Your scientists are withholding the true photographs of Mars for fear of mass hysteria. The photographs showed life on that planet.

August 28, 1965

"There will be a change of regime in China between 1967 and 1970," said the voice. "Do not believe in the pictures now being released of Mao Tse-tung. They have been faked. Mao is no longer in command, except in name."

August 31, 1965

"The United States and the Soviet Union will become allies, and practically the entire world will be the enemy of Red China after the 1980s.

"Communism was begun by a man who originally thought only good; but evil has overtaken his work. The original concept of communism was good, but the good therein has been all but discarded. The people of Russia recognize the failure of communism, and, as the years pass, they shall become more democratic.

"Before the year two thousand, there will be a unification of all religions. It can happen only after the earth has been purged of the evil force now present. A new religion will result, and this religion will be more of a philosophy than a religion in the traditional sense. The destructive characteristics of the organized religions of today shall pass away. The Roman Catholic Church, which has recognized the burning need for reform, shall emerge as a great instrument for brotherhood in the New Age. By amending its doctrines, it will neutralize its past mistakes and misdeeds and become a great force for the Light."

QUESTION: We are most interested in the child that was born in the Middle East. Can you give us more information on this?

ANSWER: The child, who shall lead the way in the Middle East, was born in Egypt. This is not without significance, as the ancient teachings of Egypt will become known and will be practiced when a giant vault, now buried in the sands of that country, is uncovered. The vault contains books on the teachings of the ancients, and these teachings will be applied to your time. These writings will become a guide for the man of the future. They were meant to be such.

September 3, 1965

QUESTION: What about such metaphysical religions as Christian Science?

ANSWER: Mary Baker Eddy was inspired by the higher forces, but mostly by the man Quimby. But she disclaimed all outside material help, saying that she received her beliefs and works without material assistance. After her book, *Science and Health*, was published, she withdrew it from circulation and added certain chapters and sentences disclaiming such things as Spiritualism and stating that the entire truth is one of mind over matter.

Basically, the teaching of Christian Science is correct, but it is only a beginning, a first step toward a divine metaphysics. To go beyond the beginning, meditation is necessary, and outside help is desirable; but Mrs. Eddy denounced both of those things. Consequently, many souls have passed on before their time because they refused such outside help as medical men would have been able to offer. If they had sought that help, they could have been cured, or at least eased of their pain.

Christian Science is based mainly on healing. But divine metaphysics is based on protection, so that healing is unnecessary. In Christian Science, thought is constantly geared to healing. Thus, in some unlearned persons, the dread of a disease may cause that disease, and such persons are then given the opportunity to cure the disease by means of Christian Science. Remember, however, that Christian Science is but a new religion, while divine metaphysics is as old as time.

September 6, 1965

QUESTION: Just how will New York City be destroyed?

ANSWER: There will be a great storm. A hurricane, with the strength and force of ten hurricanes, shall sweep up along the eastern coast of the United States and destroy much of the present shoreline by inundation.

QUESTION: How long will the war last in southern Asia?

ANSWER: This needless waste of human life will continue for at least twenty years, if not in Vietnam itself then in other parts of Southeast Asia.

QUESTION: What about Russia? What part will that country play in the future?

ANSWER: A revolution has been going on in Russia, ever so quietly, but a revolution nonetheless. The youth of Russia realize that communism cannot bring the happiness or the peace of mind for which they are searching.

The United States and Russia will be allied before 1980. The danger is Red China. Even the people of China wish to have back their ancient spiritual way of life, but those in power in that country make that impossible.

October 12, 1965

QUESTION: In the past, you've often spoken of cures. Will there ever be a cure for the common cold?

ANSWER: The cure for the common cold will take the form of a pill which will isolate and freeze the cold germ until it passes out of the system. This cure will be on the market within the next decade.

October 29, 1965

QUESTION: Many mediums have said that those who are spiritual in thought, and otherwise innocent, will have warnings of the destruction that is to come. What will those warnings be?

ANSWER: The forces of the spirit are at work, even now, giving warnings. The first warning will be changes in the weather: drought, followed by excessive rainfall. The second warning will be darkness descending upon your city. The third will be racial violence of a magnitude unparalleled in the history of man.

These warnings will come about shortly. And many things will make it impossible for any person of a spiritual or sensitive nature to exist in New York City. Materialism will become all-powerful, and horror will descend upon the city. It will be almost impossible even to venture into the streets without becoming witness to some ugliness.

November 11, 1965

QUESTION: New York has just experienced a blackout of all its electrical power. Was this the warning of darkness of which you spoke?

ANSWER: Yes. And there will be further blackouts, culmi
nating in one that shall last for three days and three
nights. This is in the distant future, and it will be among
the last of the warnings. Another warning will be trem
ors of the earth, earthquakes, that will be felt across
the country. New York will also experience these.

December 2, 1965

QUESTION: It was stated recently that archaeologists ha
discovered Noah's Ark on a mountaintop. Is this true?

ANSWER: No. The true story is that the voice heard b
Noah indicated to him a mountain and told him t
build upon it. And Noah built upon it a huge barn, i
the shape of an ark, in such a way that it would b
able to withstand the water if it rose that high. Th
animals were housed in that barn on the top of th
mountain. Naturally, those animals were the domest
cated ones of the vicinity and, in addition, some of th
wild ones native to that region. Obviously, it woul
have been impossible to gather together one pair
every species in existence. Nor was it necessary to
so, for the story of Noah and the Flood has bee
changed in the telling: the barn has become an ark, th
Flood from a localized—albeit extraordinary—one h
become a universal one.

In this story, there is one thing to remember: t
Divine Mind spoke to Noah during his meditation a
gave him that which he needed to know in order to
saved.

QUESTION: What about Adam and Eve? Did they rea
exist?

ANSWER: Actually, there was no Adam and no Eve.
life's spiritual level forms of energy or souls beca
disobedient. The earth was created and these souls w
placed upon it so that they might learn through ha
and difficult experience. Many such souls were pla
on earth at the same time, and the allegory of Ad

and Eve is merely a symbolic representation of those souls.

February 1, 1966

QUESTION: Can you clear up the mystery of Shakespeare? Did he write the plays attributed to him? Who was Bacon?

ANSWER: Shakespeare was a metaphysician. That he believed in the spiritual side of life is evidence in all his writings. He received his works through a psychic medium—and that medium was Francis Bacon. Now you understand how the controversy began.

Innate talent is always spiritual. Thus, the higher forces gave Shakespeare his plays, through Bacon. Shakespeare and Bacon were intelligent enough to remain aloof. They destroyed the original texts, and that is why so little is known. Given the beliefs of that day and age, they would have been burned at the stake if it had become known how the plays were written.

You will notice that all of Shakespeare's work deals with forces, good or bad, and spiritual, or with extraordinary happenings of some kind.

March 28, 1967

QUESTION: Do flying saucers really exist? And what are they?

ANSWER: Flying saucers do exist, and more and more of them are coming into your earth's atmosphere. Although no one on earth has yet spoken with a being from another planet, this meeting will eventually take place. Many flying saucers will be seen, and they will be seen by vast numbers of earth people. The skies will be filled with them.

Beings from other planets are carefully watching the earth, as they do not wish to have earth's erroneous thinking spread beyond your planet. For this reason, many astronauts will die, for the most part under mysterious circumstances, and the plans for space exploration of all the major powers will be set back by accidents and other occurrences. The time is not yet for your people to go forth into space; you must first conquer the ills, both physical and spiritual, that still beset the earth.

April 5, 1966

The voice said: "Fires will be another warning of the destruction that is to come. These will occur in the West, particularly along the coast of California.

"Parts of southern California will also be in the path of destruction, Los Angeles being directly in the path of earthquakes."

May 10, 1966

QUESTION: You have spoken of racial violence. Just where will this take place, and how bad will it be?

ANSWER: The areas most affected by the racial violence that is to occur within the next few years will be sections of Texas, the cities of Chicago, Cleveland, and Los Angeles, and certain areas in and around New York City. There will be many deaths, and there will be much destruction of homes and other property. Of all areas, the northeastern coast of the United States will suffer most.

QUESTION: When will this violence end? And how will it end?

ANSWER: When all races regard all others as their equals, then will the violence end, and then will the riots die of their own accord. When brotherhood is truly practiced in the cities, racial conflict will end.

That seems a far distance in the future.

August 16, 1966

QUESTION: Can you tell us what exercise is the most beneficial for one's health?

ANSWER: For your bodies, the most practical and rewarding exercise is swimming. It makes use of every muscle in the body, yet does not tax the heart. The American Indians, for example, swam to the age of ninety-eight or over. They made use of swimming as therapy as well as a preventive of sickness. It is the best exercise for circulation of the blood, and if one swam for one hour each day he would remain free of arthritis and heart ailments.

Until the Indians were placed on reservations by the white man, they were free of these diseases. Similarly, the buffalo had little disease before the white man introduced infected animals into the country; the buffalo was naturally resistant to disease.

Most animals pass disease on to human beings, but the buffalo was a purifying factor for the Indian. When a buffalo was killed, the Indian drank its blood, and his blood was purified by the purity of the buffalo's blood. Thus, even cases of extreme hemophilia cancers of the blood were able to be cured in this manner.

August 31, 1966

The voice reiterated: "There will be many fires on the western coast of the United States during the next few years, and Los Angeles will be the area most affected. Homes, property, and acres of forest land will be destroyed. This will mark the beginning of many years of destruction on the West Coast."

September 17, 1966

QUESTION: What can you tell us of the groups called "hippies"? Are they a force for good or for evil? What will come of this movement?

ANSWER: The groups that you refer to as "hippies" will be in greater evidence during the next few years, but the movement will disintegrate gradually when those who are seriously seeking spiritual enlightenment through it discover that such enlightenment can be obtained neither through drugs nor through an association with depravity.

The idea basic to the hippie movement is good, and it is from this goodness that many changes will be effected in the youth of your country. The first manifestations of that idea, however, will be so extreme in thought, action, and ideals that it will not be possible for it to advance.

One cannot advance to the higher, meditative way of life by denouncing materialism on the one hand, and, on the other, by depending upon material things such as drugs to sustain spiritual progress.

Many who follow this movement will become ill from neglect. They are not capable of handling the difficult, higher learning of India that they are trying so hard to assimilate. It has taken the wise men of India thousands of years to seek out a way to the enlightened path, to a mystic life. What has been learned so arduously cannot be copied or absorbed in a day, or a year; it is the study of a lifetime and demands years of questful study. The discipline that is necessary for such an undertaking is lacking among the hippies. Thus, these young people will turn away from it, and will take refuge in the drugs which, they feel, can give them instantly the spiritual and psychic fulfillment that they seek.

The hippie movement will die out. But it will return with a strength and an understanding that will shatter every barrier to true brotherhood and love. Then, the New Age will surely be at hand.

October 24, 1966

QUESTION: You have spoken of many cures in the near future. What about cancer? Will there be a cure for this dread disease?

ANSWER: If I were to tell you that there already exists a cure for cancer, would you believe me? There is such a cure, but it has been suppressed by your government and medical associations for the sake of the money that is being received by doctors who treat cancer victims.

This is true also of the cure to the common cold of

which we spoke in an earlier trance. The cure—although it will not be made public for a time—exists already, and it is capable of doing away with this scourge. But one must remember the billions of dollars that would not go into the pockets of the manufacturers and vendors of pills, liquids, and various forms of medications and remedies if this cure were made available.

So it is also with the war in southeastern Asia. It could be ended, but it is being sustained and escalated by a group of twenty-five or thirty business tycoons in your country.

It is because of such foulness and evil that destruction must come.

Many of the predictions made in these trance sessions have already been fulfilled. Among them are those having to do with changes in the weather (drought and then flooding in the eastern United States); the electrical blackouts (two of them, one affecting New York City); racial conflict in the areas foreseen; the setback of the United States space program (six astronauts have died in accidents during 1966 and 1967); fires in Los Angeles and its environs; and the initial disintegration of the hippie movement.

It is difficult to suppress a feeling akin to panic when I hear on television or read in the newspapers that one of my predictions has been realized, for there remain prophecies the fulfillment of which will be awesome in its implications, such as the forthcoming destruction of New York City by an incredible natural force. There are times when I devoutly wish that I am wrong, that I have misinterpreted, misstated, what the future holds. But as the prophecies, one by one, are being realized, I am losing hope that we can escape the remainder of what I have seen in our future. The only chance we have, apparently, lies in a return to spirituality and an abandonment of materialism.

If psychic talent contains in its very essence one element of agony and frustration, it is that by which the psychic is allowed to see into the future but deprived of the power to avert, or even to retard, what he sees there.

14

When I am approached with questions about the psychic world and about clairvoyance, it is usually by the young. For it is the young people of this country who are weary of materialism, of governments and religions whose sole accomplishments over the centuries have been fear, lies, hatred, war, and death. It is the young who seek the means to create a better world in rebelling against everything for which the old ways stand. It is the young who are condemned for outlandish dress and attitudes whereas, in fact, all that they are trying to do is to create an atmosphere reminiscent of the days when the world was not mechanized, computerized, push-buttoned and buttoned-down to the nth degree, when governments and people were not power- and money-crazed, when nations did not periodically and regularly send forth their sons to be torn apart on the battlefields in senseless and immoral wars. And it is the young who, despite every obstacle, will —I feel it psychically—create the world that they crave, a world of love, understanding, peace, and universal brotherhood.

The one question constantly put to me by these young, altruistic souls is, "Is it possible to develop a psychic sense? Can psychic powers be shared by everyone, so that we all can make use of them to help ourselves? Or is this an ability meant only for a chosen few?"

The answer to this question—as the reader will have gathered from the preceding chapters—is that psychic power can indeed be developed by anyone. I am convinced that everyone is psychic to some degree, though the degree may differ from person to person as does any other talent; everyone, for example, has the physical apparatus necessary for seeing, but some people see extremely well and others almost not at all. Despite such degrees of difference, it is safe to say that everyone has a certain psychic sense. Every person I have ever met has had some intuitive experience, for instance, and intuition is a psychic manifestation. We have all been in situations where we could swear we have been before, and in which we remember details about the place itself, about conversations, and so forth. Most of us have had some experience with premonitions of death, sickness or other things either good or bad, concerning someone far away, before we have learned of these events through the normal channels. Each of us has had hunches—i.e., flashes of intuitive knowledge—which we have ignored because they seemed illogical at the time; yet, we often have had occasion to say, "I could kick myself around the block for not doing what I first felt I should do about this situation."

All of these things are spontaneous (that is, uncontrolled) outward signs of the existence of a psychic or "sixth" sense. Like any sense, the psychic sense can be developed by its use in the proper way, by exercises—just as the outward eye can be strengthened by proper exercise or a musical "ear" developed by practice. And the way *par excellence* for developing one's vestigial sixth sense is by the exercise called meditation which, when practiced over a period of time, opens up, so to speak, the psychic senses and brings inner strength as well as the answer to the problems that one must confront in daily life.

The reader may perhaps remember that one of the factors that made me reluctant to take up a career as a psychic was the enormous amount of effort and discipline involved. I was lazy, and I wanted instant results without having to adopt the means necessary to attain the end. That attitude, of course, is death to the seeker after wisdom—as it is to the seeker after just about anything. It should be clearly understood at the beginning that it is absolutely impossible to evolve one's psychic senses or to attain a higher way of life merely by wishing for it, or by going at it in a desultory, off-again on-again fashion. The key to success is determination, persistence, and effort. It takes years of training, self-discipline, and meditation to develop our latent sixth sense, but it is well worth the effort.

The basic means for psychic progress is meditation, as I have said throughout this book. But what is meditation, and, specifically, what is psychic meditation? Psychic meditation is the act of looking inward, searching one's inner self, one's soul. It is a concentration on a higher Truth for the purpose of applying that Truth in all of life's situations. This Truth is one that can be possessed only when a person is at peace with himself and with the rest of the world; and one can be at peace only when one knows and understands himself and himself in relation to the world. Meditation, therefore, is aimed immediately at a knowledge of oneself, and ultimately at a knowledge of higher Truth. It is a means to an end, and not an end in itself. It must never become a ritual without meaning, as religious practices so often seem to become.

Psychic meditation, however, differs from the meditation advocated by the Christian religions in that it aims at inducing in the person meditating a state that is free of tension and free of effort. In this sense, meditation becomes the act of abstracting from one's material self, and thus allowing the higher forces to enter the mind and to give needed guidance and assistance. It is the "turning off and tuning in" about which I spoke in an earlier chapter—by virtue of which one "turns off" oneself and "tunes in" to the universe around him. In thus abstracting from oneself, a person meditating drops his defenses, his guard, the thousand masks and poses and stratagems that he uses in everyday life to protect himself from the emotional, intellectual, and physical demands made upon him by the people about him. Once this "civilized" or social veneer has been stripped away, one sees oneself as he truly is, without pretenses and without defensive mechanisms. Thus, meditation brings about, in an easy, effortless manner, a knowledge of the true self.

This illumination of the self is the blossoming of the soul; in meditation, it is as uncomplicated and as natural—and, therefore, as inevitable—as the flowering of a bud. The man who has attained to that knowledge does not have to *try* to be loving; love becomes as natural to him as, say, hate is to the hateful man. Man, in a state of self-knowledge, does not have to try to be himself; he *is* himself, and he cannot be otherwise.

Thus far, we have spoken of meditation as an act, or action. Like every action, it has a technique all its own, a technique tried in the crucible of experience, which is intended to produce the desired results with the least waste of time and energy. Here is a brief, but comprehensive, description of that technique:

1. Initially, one should choose a regular place for meditation. It should be a quiet place, as far removed from interruption as possible. This is particularly desirable for one just beginning the practice of meditation. Later on, of course, once the habit of meditation has been acquired in some degree of perfection, one is able to meditate anytime, any place.

2. Select a chair that is neither too comfortable (or you may go to sleep) nor too uncomfortable (or you will be distracted and ill at ease). Life strikes the balance between comfort and discomfort, good and evil, pleasure and pain; thus, the chair becomes a symbol of life. For the first few months, try to use the same chair. After that, use other chairs, at random, in order to acquire the ability to meditate anywhere.

3. Select a particular hour of the day for your daily meditation, a time when you are least likely to be interrupted and one that you will not have to change for one reason or another. The body and the mind both are creatures of habit, and they respond automatically to the timetable of their needs; hunger, sleep, wakefulness, etc., all are felt at one hour rather than another because all of those needs are accustomed to being satisfied at that hour. So, too, the mind will form the habit quickly enough of meditating at a particular time, and once that habit has been acquired the process will be surprisingly quick and effortless.

4. Now you must choose an object on which to concentrate during meditation. A flower will do, for example, or a candle flame. I have found candle flames particularly effective, as was evident from the accounts of my first trances. The flickering of the flame seems, for some reason, to be especially soothing. Moreover, the flame is symbolic of energy, life, and Light.

Let us suppose that you have chosen an object. Now, sit about three feet from it, and stare into its center.

Relax. Let go. Relax . . .

Become silent, really silent . . .

Silence your emotions . . .

Silence your desires . . .

Block out the exterior world, the turmoil, the problems . . .

Concentrate only on the object in front of you. Think of its beginning. If the object is a flower, as you gaze into its center think of where the flower came from.

Concentrate on its scent.

Concentrate on its color.

See it in your mind as a bud. See the leaves and petals forming. See the bush from which the flower has come, and see the earth from which the bush has sprung.

Soon, there will be nothing but the object.

Make it the only thing.

Let the mind become quiet.

Let your desires be silent.

Let the body be free and relaxed.

And then, listen . . . *listen*.

If you have attained the proper mood, you will hear the law of the universe.

If you cannot accomplish this at first, do not be discouraged. It will come after more practice. Do not give up after only a few attempts. The telephone may ring, the baby may cry, or you may be forcibly distracted in many other ways. Even your own thoughts, in the form of distractions, may interfere. But, if you work at it with persistence and courage, the voice will be heard. And even if you linger but a short time in meditation, even if you are successful in forgetting the material side of life only for a few minutes, you will experience a peace and contentment that you have never dreamed existed.

As time passes and you become more adept in concentrating, you will bring to meditation your problems and difficulties. In divine meditation, the answers and solutions will come. As surely as a psychic is able to receive impressions about others, you will be able to receive answers about yourself. In this interchange between mind, soul, and self, you will have the psychic experience of meeting your own being. Remember that a psychic merely reads what is already in the person's being, be it in his past or in his future. If the psychic is able to read the past or future of another person, you certainly should be able to read your own. But first, you must work to remove all physical, material obstacles, through unrelenting meditation. Remember that meditation, like all human acts, is a habit. And, like all habits, it is acquired very imperfectly by the first act, but with increasing perfection in subsequent acts. Perfection, even relative perfection, is attainable only by persistence and repetition.

It is important that one have the proper attitude or approach to meditation. In that respect, one should remember that the true psychic, mystic, or metaphysician does not meditate for the sake of the material things of the world, nor does he attempt to escape through meditation from his responsibilities and problems. In this, incidentally, lies my basic objection to LSD and other so-called psychedelic drugs, for they are but the means of escape from a reality which has become, to the user, overpowering. Psychic meditation, on the other hand, permits one to see the truth as it is, and it gives the inner spiritual strength necessary to go ever forward. And it accomplishes this through the strength of one's own will and mind, and without depending upon a material crutch—whether the crutch take the form of drugs, religious dogma, or other opiates that operate by demanding an abdication of the will and then by dictating a course of action.

The above notwithstanding, it must be said that in following a course of meditation and metaphysical teachings, one is bound to improve not only his spiritual life, but also his material life. Logically, it is inescapable, for the material is necessary to the spiritual in the very real sense that it is dependent upon it. Think, for example, of the various difficult situations in which you have found yourself at different times in your life. Say that you have had a disastrous "affair of the heart." Would it have ended disastrously if you had had the proper attitudes, the proper and healthy feelings not only about the other person but about yourself? That is, would it have ended badly if you had been filled with love instead of being filled with self? Probably not. Similarly, difficulties in one's professional life often are caused by one's inability to estimate objectively one's own talents and abilities; one either tends to bite off more than one can chew (and then fails), or takes on less than he can handle (and then is bored and miserable). The solution, of course, is self-knowledge at a very practical level.

So far as the disposition is concerned that one brings to meditation, it is useful to have a foundation in some branch of metaphysical learning, such as Christian Science or Yoga. This, however, is only "useful," and not necessary in the quest of spiritual truth. Only one thing is necessary: the will to gain spiritual enlightenment. You, and only you, can provide that, just as you, and only you, can experience that enlightenment.

The foregoing is a very brief description of meditation, of what one must bring to it and what one can expect to get out of it. At the risk of seeming repetitive, I should like to reiterate or restate some of the observations touched on in the course of that description.

First remember that man's psychic sense is developed to an important degree by abstracting from the material as much as is humanly possible. The ideal—indeed, the only—method for doing this effectively is through meditation. If the same result is attempted by the use of such drugs as LSD, the user may indeed experience a sense of freedom and even attain to what he regards as a glimpse of the eternal. But he has not gained freedom, he has merely escaped; for he has no control over his mind during his experience—"trip" is the accepted term—and he cannot return when he chooses. He is not his own master, but the slave of a chemical and its effects. Similarly, what he regards as the "eternal" is in reality only a figment of his mind, the effect of the chemical upon certain areas of his brain—a material phenomenon, materially produced, and similar in every way to the hallucinations of a man in the throes of advanced alcoholism. Disregarding, as being beyond our province and our competence, the physical and psychological risks involved in the use of such drugs, we may say that, from the standpoint of spiritual knowledge and advancement, LSD is not only useless but also harmful, for its use constitutes an abdication of freedom and of responsibility—and therefore a denial of the very things that spiritual progress should involve. (Remember, too, that although there may be many "dry runs" in meditation, there are no "bad trips.")

A particularly harmful form of interest in the spiritual life is that which insists on instant success. The current mad rush of celebrities to the far reaches of India in a misinformed search for psychic awareness will, as it must, end in disappointment for those concerned. It is of the essence of the spiritual life that effort and time must be involved, for there are many obstacles—to wit, the habits of a lifetime—to be overcome. If man were so little removed from spiritual perfection as to be capable of becoming an "instant mystic," then he would not be in so sad a shape as he is at present. So, unless one is prepared to devote years—a lifetime, in fact—to meditation and psychic development, he would be better off not to undertake it in the first place. Otherwise, all he will find is disillusionment and failure.

Such juvenile I-want-it-*now* attitudes are, of course, the natural fruit of general ignorance concerning the psychic world. Everything is taught in the schools and universities today, from cake-baking to world-exploding—everything, that is, except the one thing that should be taught: the development of the soul, or of the subconscious mind, and its senses. I say it is "the one thing that should be taught," because it is obvious by now, even to the most benighted pedagogue, that it is neither cakes nor cobalt bombs—nor anything in between, curricula notwithstanding—that can bring happiness to man. Only the spiritual life can give him that, along with security, knowledge, and enlightenment. The way to that spiritual life—that is, meditation and the resulting psychic experiences—go back thousands of years, to the earliest human civilizations. But for centuries these rules and systems of spiritual enlightenment were ignored by Western thinkers. Finally, the West, no longer able to cope with the monster of materialism that it has created, has begun to seek out these teachings.

Now, perhaps, a word of caution is in order. One should be aware, before undertaking a course of meditation and psychic development, that a knowledge of oneself and, possibly, of one's future does not imply that one will be able to control that future. That is, it is not difficult to foresee, psychically, an unhappy occurrence in one's life;

but one should realize that what will be will be—because it already *is*. And, therefore, one cannot expect to be able to avert what is to happen. On the other hand, the knowledge that comes from psychic development will give one the strength to face problems and difficulties, no matter how great.

In brief, then, one should not expect the impossible, even of the psychic world. But people often do. For example, many people come to me in need of help, obviously expecting to find some kind of metaphysical magician who can provide, instantly, solutions and answers to all of their problems and questions. They are doomed to disappointment. I, like any psychic, can only guide, can only attempt to shed some light on a situation which the person concerned cannot, for one reason or another, see for himself. A karmic debt, for instance—about which we spoke in the preceding chapter, in the context of "the Hoover trances"—can never be erased by anyone, under any circumstances; not by a psychic, or by a priest, doctor, or psychiatrist. It can only be done away with when it is satisfied by the person who has the obligation to do so. Moreover, there are experiences and events that we must live through for the good of our souls, and sometimes to prevent greater evils. (Recall my near-fatal accident in Georgia. I questioned its usefulness at the time, but if I had not undergone it then I surely might have been killed later in the trailer-camp mishap.)

Finally, it should be noted that the most inauspicious place in which to try to develop one's psychic senses is a modern city. The vibrations of a large city are quite low and antipathetic to psychic experiences, since they have an adverse effect on the sensitive centers of the soul, or nervous system, or subconscious. In addition to less perceptible factors, there is noise, constant interruptions, etc., all of which distract and irritate and render concentration difficult. That is not to say that it is impossible to progress spiritually in a large city. Tibetan monks, for example, learn to meditate sitting alongside an ever-clanging bell, and in time they reach a state of detachment that enables them to be oblivious to the sound. Those good men, however, have no occupation other than learning to meditate. Few of us are so fortunate. Nonetheless, if one is able to begin in a quiet place, then he should be able to go out into the world and continue to meditate wherever he may be. It is difficult in the early stages of development, but it becomes easier as one progresses. It is quite easy to be wholly spiritual at a time of peace and quiet, but it is the time of strife and hardship that separates the men from the boys in the world of the psychic.

I realize that I have only touched on the most basic aspects of psychic development. It would require many books to satisfy all the requirements of everyone who wishes to begin to make progress in the spiritual life, and this brief autobiography is not intended for that purpose. All that I wished to point out was that every human being can develop his psychic abilities, and I hope that this short explanation of how to begin doing so will prove useful to those who have the interest and the courage to walk in the path of Truth. The way is a long and arduous one, but it is more than worth the effort.

Epilogue

The lot of a professional psychic, as I have explained, is not always a happy one. Besides skepticism and outright condemnation, there are other adverse conditions a psychic must contend with in his day-to-day existence.

It is a fact that the psychic is forced, by his own physical limitations, to withhold his gift from many people who need his help and ask for it. During the first nine months of 1967, for example, I received thousands of requests for private consultations but could reach only a very small percentage of these as there was not the time or the strength to do more. Psychic work has depleted me to such an extent that on many occasions I have had to take a break from it for weeks because of complete exhaustion which overtook me.

Also, the responsibility of being a psychic is a tremendous one. In the early part of 1968 I gave a lecture-demonstration at the renowned Town Hall in Manhattan and it was attended by more than a thousand persons, most of whom came for a psychic message of some kind. During the section of the lecture when I go into the audience and give short psychic impressions, I went up into the balcony and was soon confronted by a crowd of people who gathered around me pleading for answers to their questions. The gathering turned into a mob and they were uncontrollable. It was, to say the least, frightening. Fortunately I had taken someone with me and we were able to fend off the crowd and return to the comparative safety of the backstage area. While I had been in the midst of the crushing throng, a woman of about sixty years of age took hold of my arm and pleaded with me.

"Mr. Logan," the lady asked, "I have recently had an operation for cancer. Will it return?"

The lady repeated the question several times. In a flash

I felt that she indeed would not be free of this affliction, but I could not bring myself to tell her this. I could sense that she was seeking a confirmation of her own hopes—that the dreaded disease would not return. I didn't answer. However, no matter where I turned, this lady was facing me, demanding an answer to her question. Finally I told her that the disease would not return. I knew that if I had given her the truth, she would not have been able to take it. This was one of the few times that I have not been completely truthful with my psychic gift. I point out this incident to show what a responsibility a psychic has.

And what does the future have in store for Daniel Logan? I shall herewith give the reader a look into the coming events in my own life.

In 1968 I was asked to lecture at both New York University and Hunter College in New York. I shall put such lectures foremost in my work as I feel the education of those interested in the subject is of the most importance at this time. Also, I shall continue radio and television appearances, such as the ones I have recently done in New York for Alan Burke and Long John Nebel, both men who not only have interesting, informative shows, but who have done a lot in bringing before the public those with experience in parapsychology and related fields.

Although I must cut down even more on my personal consultations, because they have become so depleting, I realize that this will always be a part of my work, as it is the consultations which have done the most good. In the past few months I have given consultations to many various kinds of people—from the gifted comedienne Peggy Cass to the magazine and publishing tycoon Gardner Cowles and members of his family, from a poverty-striken family in Brooklyn to an ill and outcast member of society in the Bahamas.

In the next few years I shall go to Japan, and other sections of the Orient, and study the different religions and philosophies of these countries, with the hope of advancing my own spiritual worth. I feel that I have not given myself the needed opportunity to develop my own soul and this I feel I must do. I don't wish to gain the world and lose myself in the process. I have chosen the Orient because I feel, as stated in an earlier chapter, that I have lived in these places before, in another lifetime. I hope to delve into the world of reincarnation. I intend to go into a Buddhist monastery and afford myself some time to learn more about myself and the world within.

Finally, with all my strength and ability, I will help the youth of the world in its struggle to end hatred, war, and selfishness so that the "New Age" of which the voices have spoken may indeed come to pass—that time of which it is said in the Book of Revelation, "There will be no more death, and no more mourning or sadness. The world of the past is gone."

I have found that it is only in the world of the spiritual that there is not death or sadness. I hope that this book has succeeded in arousing at least an interest in the question of whether or not there exists something other than the material world. From my own experiences I am convinced that there is a reality far greater than the material, but it is up to each individual to seek and to find the answers himself.

May your search be fruitful.

Afterword
for the
AVON EDITION

A greater acceptance of, and belief in, psychic phenomena has swept over the United States since the hard cover edition of this book was published. Unlike the "occult fad," which took place in the 1930's, this new interest in the various phases of parapsychology is of a lasting quality. I see this as the beginning of "the Age of Aquarius" (materiality is on the wane, even though it is putting up a final, violent struggle). All around me I discover those seeking spiritual enlightenment and unfoldment. I would venture to say that nine out of ten people with whom I come into contact today express some kind of interest in one or more aspects of psychic phenomena.

On lecture tours across the country, I have listened to hundreds, more likely thousands, of stories that have a basic psychic foundation, told to me by people who previously either shrugged off this kind of experience or else kept it to themselves for fear of being labeled "strange." There has been an emergence of those with abilities related in some way to the psychic world and it is now not uncommon to find even heads of corporations utilizing the talents of mediums, astrologers and the like. Unfortunately, the crackpots and fakes are getting as much coverage as the well intentioned in these fields.

In the spring of 1969, while I was in California on one of my tours, I was asked to give my psychic viewpoint on "the great earthquake" which was to occur along the San Andres fault, devastating much of California by causing it to break away from the mainland and to sink into the ocean. Many psychics and star-gazers agreed with the predictions of destruction originally made by an internationally known lady psychic and a New York City TV astrologer-medium, who had gone as far as giving two alternate dates for the catastrophe—April 4 or April 19,

1969. On either of these dates, so they felt, California would be no more.

Most of the nation treated California's projected demise with a sense of humor—there were two bestselling songs, a bestselling novel and countless jokes, all based on the end of California. Upon my arrival in Los Angeles and San Francisco, however, I found the local residents taking the matter anything but lightly. In actual fact, there was widespread fear and in some instances, feelings akin to panic had overtaken entire townships.

My own psychic impression was that there would be no major earthquake in April of 1969. I felt that what many of the true psychics (as opposed to those who got on the bandwagon) had sensed were the horrendous mud slides and the innundation which had happened along the southern California coast during the early months of 1969. I have predicted that southern California would someday be destroyed—but this is an eventual occurrence, over a long period of time. California will not crumble into the ocean at a given instant. I sense a gradual geological change on the west coast of the United States. Earthquakes will strike California (you don't have to be psychic to predict that) and it will be after countless years, and after many warnings, that the geological change will take place whereby the shape of California is altered.

April 4 and April 19, 1969 came and went with barely a tremor in California.

What was the impression I received of California on my second visit there? As you recall, I had only bad "vibrations" during my first visit to the city of Los Angeles. I felt, from many conversations on this second trip, that the fear of oncoming destruction had forced a major portion of the population to veer from the materialism which I had previously sensed in the very air (smog) of Los Angeles itself.

I had more positive psychic impressions about California this time, most specifically in regard to its youth. I also had the opportunity to meet numbers of persons involved in the making of films and in the TV industry. They appeared to be more advanced types (spiritually) than those who preceded them. Many of the creative individuals in California are beginning to become involved in expressing qualities they have only recently discovered within themselves—positive, metaphysical, non-material feelings.

In a much lighter vein, at about the same time as the earthquake talk, I was asked to give my impressions as to who would win the Academy Awards for 1968. I actually do not like to give such predictions, as it is almost impossible to do—very much like horse races. I was not asked my thoughts on some of the awards, but on *all* of them. As I became better known, the press, TV and radio interviewers, and the public demanded a higher degree of accuracy—in any given situation.

Three years before the 1968 Academy Awards, I had sensed that Barbra Streisand would win the award for best actress. The prediction appears earlier in this book, and was written two years before the 1968 Academy Awards presentations. When I first made the prediction, many of my own friends told me that it would not see fruition because Miss Streisand would most probably not ever make a motion picture. At that time, there was much ridiculous talk that she would not photograph well.

I not only said that Barbra Streisand would be a success in films but that she would win an Academy Award for her initial performance in a motion picture. I think that such an impression can be counted as a psychic feeling if it does indeed turn out to be as predicted—much more so than my giving a list of the twenty-seven winners in the various catagories a week before the occasion.

On December 27, 1968 (and repeated in February of 1969) I appeared on the *Long John Nebel Show*, NBC. Mr. Nebel asked me who I felt would be the winners this year as I had accurately predicted 90% of the winners the previous year. The nominations for the awards, as of that date, had not been announced.

I said that the best film award would go to either *The Lion In Winter* or *Oliver*. I felt that the best actress award would also be very close that year and predicted Barbra Streisand (*Funny Girl*) or Katharine Hepburn (*The Lion In Winter*) would take home the coveted statue. (*Oliver* did win and for the first time in the history of the Awards, two actresses tied for the Best Actress Award—Barbra Streisand and Katharine Hepburn!)

Ironically, I had stated that the New York Film Critics Award (another important film award) would not go to either of the ladies I mentioned for the Oscar, but rather to Joanne Woodward for the film, *Rachel, Rachel*. Miss Woodward did win this award.

As the weeks approached the actual voting, I was forced by the skeptics and the communications people into choosing only one winner in each category. I went along with this demand knowing that it was almost an impossibility. I was proven wrong in several instances because of the pressure placed on me to be more specific. But, I learned a dear lesson from it—I don't know everything and could not have a psychic impression about everything. I was wrong that year in regard to the Best Actor. I know that Peter O'Toole will win an award eventually and felt that it would be for his acting in *The Lion In Winter*. I still feel that Mr. O'Toole will indeed win an award in the near future, very possibly for his role in the musical version of *Goodbye, Mr. Chips*, which, at this writing, is still to be completed and released.

In the early part of 1967, I had been introduced to Ira Levin at a party in New Jersey. I told him that my feeling was that he would be most happy with the outcome of the film version of his best seller, *Rosemary's Baby*. I predicted the film to be a tremendous success and an award winner.

A month prior to the world premiere of *Rosemary's Baby* (on the ABC TV network—*The Dick Cavett Show*) I predicted that Ruth Gordon would win the supporting actress award for her acting in *Rosemary's Baby*. She won not only the Oscar but the Golden Globe as well. The film has been internationally acclaimed and a great money maker.

Incidentally, I had a personal choice for the best supporting actress of 1968—I had personally hoped that Lyn Carlin, in the film, *Faces*, would be the winner. As I've stated before, in many instances my own feelings are distinct from the psychic impressions I receive.

Looking ahead, I have recently had the psychic feeling that Katharine Hepburn would be the first actress to win a fourth Academy Award. Miss Hepburn will be the actress to beat in the 1969 presentations. This will be for her acting in a film which is (as of this writing) neither completed nor released—*The Madwoman of Chaillot*. This film will be the recipient of several awards, not only in the United States, but in other countries as well.

Barbra Streisand, I feel, will be nominated for more films and eventually win a second award. She will be an outstanding success in films that will be straight comedies and dramas, non-singing roles.

In the summer of 1968, I said that the Jets would become the world champions in football during the 1968-69 season. Those of my sports-loving friends warned me not to make this prediction. They said that it was impossible, and I was also offered upwards of $1,000 in bets from radio interviewers. To the surprise of the entire sports world (not to me, as I know nothing about football) the Jets, with the help of Joe Namath, went on to win the title.

I have related experiences where my psychic ability has gotten me into difficulty, especially on TV and radio shows. It happens often. Dick Cavett, a bright young comedian (who also got his start as a performer at the night club I owned in Greenwich Village) was made the host of the ABC-TV series I mentioned heretofore in this chapter. Don Silverman, whose experience with me opened the first pages of this book (re the blue car incident) was the producer of this show.

Don felt that I would become a regular on the program, appearing several times per month. I did appear three times before I was suddenly, with no apparent reason, dropped from the company. I considered these shows to be my best TV appearances, as I was completely relaxed and made at ease by Don and his young, bright staff. Naturally, I became quite uptight about being let go.

For several weeks I persisted in calling Don, hoping to be given an explanation. He finally answered my plea. It seemed that on the final program of the three shows I did with Mr. Cavett, I told him something I felt would happen to him in the future.

"My impression is," I said, "that within a year or so, Johnny Carson will not be with the *Tonight Show*, and you will be his replacement!"

Mr. Cavett turned absolutely ashen, and I must admit I was quite surprised, as I had not thought of this a moment previous to its having entered my mind. The audience applauded its approval of the prediction. Mr. Cavett quickly changed the subject. I had taken this as being shyness on his part. When I was told the reason for my not being rebooked on the show, I understood Mr. Cavett's sudden deviation from the topic at hand. It wasn't shyness.

"You see," Don explained, sounding a bit embarrassed by the situation, "Dick would very much like to be the one to replace Carson, if and when the opportunity would arise. In fact, you might say that he is being groomed for this spot. Dick is a close friend of Carson's and he felt that if the Carson staff heard of your prediction, it would cause friction between the two of them, or worse—they might interpret the prediction as not a psychic impression, but as our getting points across to the network."

Thus, I did not re-appear on the *Dick Cavett Show*. The final outcome of the Cavett-Carson prediction remains to be seen, although it may already have. Dick Cavett has replaced Johnny Carson as the host of *The Tonight Show* on more than a number of occasions since I made the prediction—he had not done so previous to that. Could these few instances be what I had been receiving psychically? Or will Dick Cavett take Johnny Carson's place on a more permanent basis in the future? Tune in next week to The Further Troubles Of A Psychic!

Another example of saying too much of what I sense without giving forethought (which is the best way in which I work over the air) took place in Minneapolis, Minnesota. I was interviewed by the host of a well known local TV show.

"I feel that you have one child," was the impression I had about the man.

Although he confirmed my other impressions, he told me that he had two children. I nevertheless felt quite positive that I had been right in sensing him to be the father of only one child, but of course he was adamant.

"Well, I have been wrong before," I said, conceding defeat. "It's just that it was such a definite impression."

When the show ended, the host took me aside and told

me that in reality he was the father of only one child, but that he and his wife had adopted a second child (who might possibly have been watching the program) and he did not wish this child to know of the adoption.

I often wonder on how many other occasions I have inadvertently touched a delicate or personally sensitive area and have been flatly told that I was wrong.

During the three appearances I did do on the *Dick Cavett Show*, other interesting events took place. On the second program, one of the panel members was Alan Dulles. I refused to tell this man anything about himself. I just did not see a future for him—it was like looking at a blank, white card. Months later, Alan Dulles was dead.

Ethel Merman was a guest on the third and final *Dick Cavett Show* that I did. Miss Merman was one of the kindest and the most sensitive people I have encountered in show business.

"I feel that you will be offered a part in a motion picture which will be very different from the kind of thing you usually are asked to do. It will be a dramatic role; there will be no singing connected with this part. Also, I do not feel that it will be a major role, but I feel that you should accept this part when it is offered to you as your performance in it would bring about a change in your career; many doors would open for you in different directions."

Miss Merman, with that great, brassy voice of hers said, "Oh, Yes! That would be swell!"

A day or so later, while in a conversation with Miss Merman on the phone, she said, "Daniel, you're spooky! I was offered a role just like the one you said. It is a non-singing part, not too big, and is very dramatic. If I accept, it will show a different Ethel Merman. Because of your ability to see this, I am seriously considering doing it, where I might have overlooked it before."

On one of the Cavett shows, I turned to Mr. Cavett and told him that I felt he was looking for a home: that he was in the market for a house.

"But no one knows this except my wife and myself!" he protested. "It's true, we were house-hunting a few days ago."

"My further impression is that you were looking at this house in New York," I continued.

"Yes!" was his shocked reply.

"Was it in this area? Long Island or the Bronx—something like that?" I inquired.

He actually gulped.

"I feel that the initial of the town where you saw this house is either an 'M' or an 'N.'"

Mr. Cavett, amazed, agreed that this was true.

It was announced, months later in an interview with Mr. Cavett (the *New York Times*), that he had purchased a home in Montauk, Long Island. This was one of the few times when an actual letter formed in my consciousness.

At the end of each year, on the *Long John Nebel Show*, besides giving my impressions of Academy Award winners, Mr. Nebel asks me to give my prognostications for the following twelve-month period. In December of 1967, he asked me about the political future of Robert Kennedy.

"There will never be another Kennedy in the White House," was my answer.

The reaction of Mr. Nebel's other guests was combined disbelief. In December of 1967, Robert Kennedy's star was shining brightly in the political firmament, and he was the one most talked of as being the Democratic nominee for President. Many felt that he had no competition in the Presidential race.

I gave no explanation over the air as to why I felt this, but said afterwards that if Robert or Ted went toward the White House, they too would be murdered. At a lecture I gave in 1965 at Carnegie Hall, I had made the prediction that there would be two more tragedies in the Kennedy family.

At a lecture in Town Hall, February 1968, I singled out David Kahn for a brief psychic impression. Mr. Kahn is very much involved with the Edgar Cayce foundation—having been one of Mr. Cayce's close friends and the man present at most of the Cayce trance sessions.

"I feel that you will go South in the near future, but you will have to stay much longer than you planned." My immediate impression was that the delay would be caused by illness, but trying to keep positive, I avoided saying this.

Months later, Mr. Kahn and his charming wife had me to their town house in Manhattan for a visit with them. Mr. Kahn told me that he hadn't understood the message when I gave it, but that he had gone South shortly after my prediction, had become ill, and had undergone an operation. He decided to recuperate at his family's home in the South.

When we were alone, his wife having left the room to bring us something to drink, Mr. Kahn turned to me and asked if I knew how long he would be alive. I usually refuse to answer this question, but since Mr. Kahn completely understood the teachings of Karma, life after death, and as he had worked so closely with Mr. Cayce, I felt he had to know—in order to prepare for the transition.

"I will not give you a date, but I feel that you already know the time is close," I said.

"Yes, I do know this and knowing it gives me the opportunity to get things in order." He wasn't at all frightened by the idea and maintained a marvelous composure.

A few months passed and I received word that David Kahn had died.

A psychic occurrence of a much lighter nature took place when I was a mystery guest on the TV show, *What's My Line?* Having been "guessed," I was asked to demonstrate my ability for the panel members. One of the panelists was the comic Soupy Sales.

"I have an impression that you reside at one of the two addresses which I have written on this piece of paper," I said, having done this a moment before.

Soupy crossed over to my chair and said that the street was correct on one of the numbers I had written down.

"I really don't know what this means, and I don't wish to bring you bad news, but I have the impression that the police will be at the door of this place." I didn't receive anything else about it and felt a bit strange delivering such a message.

Soupy laughed. "I know what this means. The police have already come to the door of my house just the other day," he explained. "My kids play their rock and roll music too loudly and one of the neighbors finally complained to the police. The cops arrived shortly after the complaint was registered. But, no one knows this, it wasn't reported in any of the media. Now everyone knows!"

While I was on one of the four national tours I did promoting the hardcover edition of this book, I had the chance to meet with many of the publisher's representatives in the various cities. Dan Long was the representative in Houston, Texas. He and his wife were most hospitable. Mrs. Long had one child when I met them.

"I have the impression that you will have another child within the next year and a half," I told them.

Mrs. Long smiled and said, "I would like to think you are correct in your predictions, but I must tell you that the doctors have all agreed that I can never have another child. It is physically impossible. Let's say this falls in your 20% inaccuracy." I could tell that I made upset the lady quite a bit by predicting the impossible.

Four months later, I received a letter from Houston. It stated that Mrs. Long was indeed pregnant, much to the delighted surprise of the Longs and their doctors.

In the last few years, I have been involved with many incidents which prove to me the ideas behind Karma. There are people we meet with whom we have had some previous experiences. I am sure of this. One such instance occurred in 1967 at one of my lectures. A young lady, Barbara Sue Weprin, was a member of the audience. For a fleeting moment after the lecture, we spoke. Although our meeting was cordial, I never felt that I would see her again.

Some time later, I was asked to be the guest of the new TV show starring Carol Reed. It was to be taped at the Americana Hotel, in New York City. The hotel's night club, called the Royal Box, was designated as the place where we were to do the taping of the show. Immediately following the taping, two young ladies approached me from the side lines. One of them was Barbara Sue Weprin.

"How did you know I was going to be here?" I asked. "I didn't even know where they were going to tape until I arrived at the hotel. There were no announcements to the public and the show doesn't have a live audience."

"Well," Barbara said, "its really strange. I was on my lunch hour walking around with my girl friend. We had come many blocks, window shopping, and then started looking for a ladies' room. My girl friend said that there must be one in the Americana Hotel and so we came inside. The nearest ladies' room was next to the Royal Box. I was waiting for my friend in the hall and had a sudden urge to go inside the night club, even though I knew it was closed in the daytime. There was a man standing inside the door and I asked him if I could come inside. He replied that a TV show was in the midst of being filmed, but said that he supposed it would be all right for us to go in. I was truly surprised to find you doing the show. I think it's too much of a coincidence for this to be happen by chance."

Barbara and I became friends after this and we have had numerous instances of telepathy passing between us. At the exact moment of typing this paragraph, for example, Barbara called me. We speak on the average of twice or three times a month, but never at any regular time. Barbara said she had the impulse to call me from the office where she works. She has become a serious student of hand analysis (palmstry). She has already become the best hand analyst I have yet encountered. I have such a close kinship with Barbara, we seem to have shared a complete understanding and acceptance of each other's idiosyncrasies from the time we met. No one can tell me that we have not encountered one another somewhere along the way, in another time, in another situation.

Many of the original predictions made in the hardcover edition of this book, written in 1966 and 1967, have already seen fruition:

Barbra Streisand's Academy Award.

The temporary bombing halt in the Vietnam war, prior to the 1968 elections, for political reasons. (Exact statement.)

The flooding conditions throughout most of the United States (when written, drought was prevalant), the spring of '68 and '69 being the worst.

The continuing war in Southern Asia and the involvement of the United States. (Since 1966, psychics and those in related occult fields have predicted its end—I felt that it would continue for many years, and it has.)

The gradual alliance between the United States and

Russia, joining forces eventually to fight Red China. (Russia and China are now in the midst of open military action on their borders.)

The change of weather; no more Spring or Fall—extreme climate changes from hot to cold. (A majority of the cities I have visited in the past year have complained of the weather changes.)

The devaluation of money (gold). (England, as predicted, was the first and the USA will follow. The depression I predicted for the early 70's in the United States now seems like a reality—the rate of interest at an all time high, the rise in price of the cost of living reaching completely out of proportion.

The impressions that there is life on other planets. H_2O has been proven to be in the atmosphere on Mars, meaning a likelihood of life there.

On a *Long John Nebel Show* in December, 1968 I made the following new predictions:

— Politics—a very bad year (1969) for the Nixon administration. In fact, the four years of his office will be regarded as being far less effective and meaningful than the previous four under Johnson—in civil rights movements and youth movements especially. The school situation will become very bad (at the time, the trouble had just begun) and will filter down into the high school level.

— There will be no assassinations of major public figures in 1969.

— The USA will circle the moon safely and be the first to do so. (The USA did circle safely.)

— The mid-eastern situation will shortly get out of hand, and I do not feel this situation will calm down for years to come. Major trouble spot here with much bloodshed and complete warfare. (There were no disturbances at the time.)

— Worst snow in many parts of the United States in 1969, resulting in great flooding. (This happened in the mid west and northeastern states during April and May.)

— The death of one or two ex-presidents of the United States. (Former President Eisenhower died in the early spring of 1969.)

— "The Great White Hope" will be the play which will

win most of the theatrical awards. (The play won both the coveted Tony Award and the Pulitzer Prize.)

— 1969 will see an upsurge in the black-white problem, with the summer of '69 especially bad.

— Jacqueline Kennedy Onassis will be divorced within two years. I feel that she will be married three times and have three children (possibly a child with Onassis). (Some of my friends now interpret the "yacht experience" earlier in this book as referring to the Onassis yacht, with the warning to Jacqueline having new significance.)

— The cancer cure (preventive) is about to be announced and will be on the market in the early '70's.

I think the most depressing psychic impression I have ever had was one recent feeling that came to me while I was in meditation. It was so strong and so disturbing that I was ill for days. Concentrating on the Vietnam war, which never seems to end and which I predicted would not come to an end even when the United States government changed hands, I was filled with the hideous psychic thought that there would always be a Vietnam—there would, from this time on, always be a place where the major powers of the earth would fight out their differences! There would never be an all-out Atomic War, but always a battle ground! Oh, God, how I hope this prediction is wrong! How sad that we have come to this.

Everyone asks me how those of us who will be around for the next sixty to a hundred years will live through the predictions I have made. I am presently writing a book on this exact subject, based on my predictions. But we must all remember one thing—an impression *can* be changed. Example: I once told a lady that on the following Friday she would be run over by a yellow car. The lady was so frightened that she stayed in bed the entire day. On Saturday the lady called me and said, "You were wrong, Mr. Logan! I didn't get run over by a yellow car yesterday!"

"What did you do Friday?" I asked.

"I stayed in bed and covered my head with the blanket," was her reply.

The lady changed the impression. Had she gone out, she might very well have been run over as I predicted.

But she did something to change the prediction. This can happen.

A psychic, as I've said before, sees the *strongest* possibility of an outcome in a given situation. That is why it is impossible for any psychic to bat a thousand.

If the individual has a choice, so do cities, countries, the world itself. How I pray that all my negative impressions do not see fruition and that all the positive ones will come to pass. Recently, a member of a rock and roll group wrote me a letter. His name is Ralph Parrett, and he writes the words and music for the group. His vibrations are of a high level and in one of his letters he enclosed his beliefs, which he calls "An Affirmation of Life." I pass his words on to you, hoping that all of us can someday live by them. I am convinced more than ever before that our youth shall be victorious over materialism. Despite the violent, difficult times ahead we shall all overcome, we shall survive, and we shall win.

An Affirmation of Life

There are two forces at work in the universe. It is this simple: There is positivity and negativity.

Anything which is detrimental to the Life Force and evolution of man is a negative vibration, or negative energy. It takes away from LIFE.

Anything which stimulates growth or enhances life is a positive vibration, or positive energy.

The simple truth is that each and every man has the Divine power to give off positive or negative vibrations, each of which will attract its likeness.

When a man discovers that he has the power to control his vibrations, regardless of everything around him, he has begun to learn his divinity.

Many people feel that they are at the mercy of fate, and therefore spend most of their time in fear, worry and doubt regarding the things around them. In doing this, they detract from the pursuit of life, and their ability to love and enjoy life dwindles.

Fear is the strongest negative vibration, and has been used for centuries to hinder evolution. It is responsible for all sickness of mind and body. As a man spends his thoughts in fear of sickness, he releases energy capable of creating sickness. As a man begins to cast off fears, worries and doubts, and begins to replace them with positive thoughts, he learns about the power within. He begins to realize that he can control his future. No man can ever be sick in body without first having been sick in mind. No man can ever be healthy in body without first having been healthy in mind.

Knowing this, I willfully here and now affirm life. I realize that I alone am responsible for my destiny and must not blame anyone else.

I choose to understand all peoples and not to fear them. I choose to emit LOVE, the highest positive vibration, for everyone, including those I may feel wish my destruction. I realize that in striving for a continual state of love for all people and things, I am raising my vibrations and putting myself in greater control of my destiny.

War will not cease until people cast off fear and say "I will not kill." It must begin here and now with me. There is no pure state of hatred. Hatred is the guise of fear, and the man who believes that he hates does not know himself. We are all brothers and sisters, and in the bedrock of our souls wish love for each other. It is only our confusion and fear which prevents us from openly declaring this love.

I believe in touching and looking into the eyes as a form of communication.

I believe in the beauty and divinity of making love. Contrary to conventional Western belief, it is good for the soul and makes the body peaceful. I choose to love my own body as well, and to admire it often, for it is the temple of the soul.

I affirm LIFE and all its joys.

Christ taught that whatever a person believes, it shall be done unto him. Buddha said that man is the sum total of all his thoughts. Life can be filled with joy or sorrow, depending on man. I choose to Love.